THE HIP HOP GENERATION

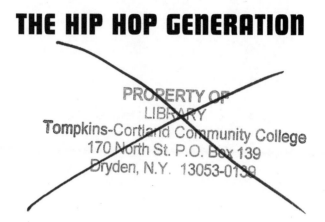

THE
HIP HOP
GENERATION

YOUNG BLACKS AND
THE CRISIS IN AFRICAN
AMERICAN CULTURE

Bakari Kitwana

BASIC
CIVITAS
BOOKS

A Member of the Perseus Books Group

Published by BasicCivitas Books,
A Member of the Perseus Books Group

Designed by Trish Wilkinson
Set in 10.5 Palatino by The Perseus Books Group

A cataloging-in-publication record for this book is
available from the Library of Congress.
ISBN 0-465-02978-7; pbk ISBN 0-465-02979-5
First Paperback Edition

04 / 10 9 8 7 6 5 4 3

For my son, Akindele Elijah Kitwana,
and his generation. May our generation provide
yours a worthy foundation on which to
build magnificent tomorrows.
And in memory of my father, Sam Dance.

Each generation out of relative obscurity must discover their mission, fulfill it or betray it.
— Frantz Fanon
The Wretched of the Earth

CONTENTS

x   *Contents*

Part 2
Confronting the Crises in African American Culture

PREFACE

OUR YOUTH CAN BE OUR FATE OR OUR FUTURE. IF YOUNG PEOPLE EMBRACE BLACK CULTURE, GROUND THEMSELVES IN IT, AND FEEL COMPELLED TO CONTINUE THE LEGACY, THEN THEY ARE OUR FUTURE. BUT IF THEY TURN THEIR BACKS ON THEIR BLACKNESS, IF THEY HAVE CONTEMPT FOR THEIR FATHERS AND MOTHERS, IF THEY DO NOTHING BUT ENGAGE IN SELF-CONGRATULATORY NARRATIVES AND MUSIC ABOUT THEMSELVES AND IMAGINE THAT THEY ARE ACTUALLY ANY THREAT TO THIS SOCIETY OR THAT THEY HAVE ANY FUTURE IN IT SIMPLY BY TALKING NEGATIVE, THEN THEY ARE NOT OUR FUTURE; THEY ARE OUR FATE.
—MAULANA KARENGA, INTERVIEW IN
The Source, FEBRUARY 1996

UNDERSTANDING THE NEW CRISES IN AFRICAN AMERICAN culture that have come about in my generation's lifetime—high rates of suicide and imprisonment, police brutality, the generation gap, the war of the sexes, Blacks selling Black self-hatred as entertainment, among others—I often wonder what life will be like for the generation of African Americans that follows. This question has been a defining one for those of us who grew up in post–civil rights Black America, especially for our generation's intellectuals. What will be our generation's contribution to the centuries-long African American struggle for liberation, and how do we redefine this struggle for our time? Our parents' achievements (the civil rights and Black power movements) continue to overshadow our lives as we struggle to answer these questions and define our generation's own identity and distinctiveness.

Although old racial stereotypes, beliefs, and practices die hard—largely in part because America is still trapped by an unreconciled racial history—we've unquestionably inherited a new America. This crazy, brave new world has spun on its head old ideas of race and America. The struggle for liberation in our generation is no longer just a Black thing. America is a more multicultural society than ever, and regardless of the fact that Blacks have become a political force, they can no longer go it alone. Even though Black-specific issues persist and America remains polarized around Black-white race relations, the old paradigms no longer apply. Coalition-building with America's other racial and ethnic groups is more critical, and viable, for our generation than for any previous generation of African Americans. At the same time, our generation of African Americans must come to grips with the damage we do ourselves in popular culture (rap lyrics and 'hood films) and in everyday life (inadequate parenting, resentment-filled interpersonal relationships, and inferior educational performance), which stands counter to traditional ideas of Blackness.

Although hip-hop, arguably the single most significant achievement of our generation, is the most visible place these issues are elucidated, it only hints at the answers we seek to the great racial questions of our time. The essence of today's Black youth culture lies much deeper than the basic elements of hip-hop culture, and it is the area beyond the music, break dancing, graffiti, dj-ing, style, and attitude that is the focus of this book.

The Hip-Hop Generation explores new attitudes and beliefs of young Blacks, examines where we are going, and analyzes the sociopolitical forces that have shaped us. While this is a book about Black youth culture that often refers to "hip-hop culture" and "hip-hop generation," it is not a book about rap music or the hip-hop industry's insiders. The term "hip-hop generation" is used interchangeably with Black youth culture. No other term better defines this generation of Black youth, as the entire spectrum of Black youth (including college students and young professionals, as well as the urban masses) has come to identify with hip-hop's cadence.

During the mid-1990s, as head editor of *The Source: the magazine of hip-hop music culture and politics*, I began to use the term "the hip-hop generation" to define our generation. Around that time, the label Generation X began to be loosely applied to young twenty-somethings, white and Black alike. Just as Black baby boomers were mostly defined by the civil rights and Black power movements, Black twenty-somethings were more than just Generation Xers in Black face. At the same time, the term "hip-hop nation" was en vogue. Hip-hop kids did not represent a nation any more than they were carbon copies of white Generation Xers. In response, those of us at *The Source* began to use the phrase "the hip-hop generation" to refer to our specific generation. It was our attempt to bring critical focus to the issues that defined our time and that went beyond simply rap music.

I have established the birth years 1965–1984 as the age group for the hip-hop generation. However, those at the end of the civil rights/Black power generation were essentially the ones who gave birth to the hip-hop movement that came to define the hip-hop generation, even though they are not technically hip-hop generationers. The Africa Bambaataas, Grandmaster Flashes, Melle Mels, Kool DJ Hercs, as well as hip-hop journalists like Nelson George and even hip-hop moguls like Russell Simmons, belong to what writer and activist Lisa Sullivan calls the "bridge generation." Those folks, who were right at the cusp, were too young to be defined by civil rights/Black power and too old to be deemed hip-hop generationers. Nonetheless, they have played a pivotal role in this generation's development by linking both.

Furthermore, although I believe that the hip-hop phenomenon has been a defining element for this entire age group (those born between 1965 and 1984), I would argue that there are probably three distinctive subgroups within this generation. Those at the beginning of the age group have a vastly different interpretation of hip-hop music, for example, than those at the end. Each subgroup undoubtedly thinks that they were the first ones who really grew up on hip-hop (but that's another story). Older hip-hop generationers may find a rapper like KRS-One or LL Cool J to be more representative of their idea of hip-hop than someone younger, who may see their hip-hop truths in, say, the Hot Boys or Lil' Bow Wow. Someone in the middle of the age group may be stuck on Wu-Tang Clan. The same is true of the sociopolitical issues that have swept the landscape and ultimately defined our lives. Individuals may point to different defining events, but all share a crystal clear understanding of coming of age in an era of post-segregation and global economics.

This exploration began with my earlier work *The Rap on Gangsta Rap*, where I begin to hone in on the idea of the hip-hop generation and the emergence of a distinctive Black youth culture. Since that 1994 publication, much of my work has centered on trying to get at the heart of the worldview of the hip-hop generation. For much of this inquiry into the hip-hop generation, I have relied on my own memory and the memories of close friends and associates as starting points. I've fleshed the rest out with lots of observation, research, and reporting over the past seven years. As executive editor turned national affairs editor at *The Source* between 1995–1999, I wanted to use the magazine's influence to change the national conversation about young Blacks, so that the discussion of hip-hop went beyond the music and the cultural movement to consider the sociopolitical forces that birthed the generation itself. It was my hope that within that more enlightened climate we could find ways to empower our generation and effect positive social change.

If we can do this, and I remain unshaken in my belief that we can, the next generation of African American youth can move beyond the crises of our time and embrace their own era in an America true to its promise of equality and inclusion. *The Hip-Hop Generation* is a contribution to that effort.

ACKNOWLEDGMENTS

THIS BOOK WAS INSPIRED IN MANY WAYS BY THE WRITINGS, analyses and cultural criticism of Maulana Karenga, Kalamu ya Salaam, Cornel West, bell hooks, Michael Eric Dyson, Acklyn Lynch, Ishmael Reed, Adolph Reed and countless other Black intellectuals who've expanded the range of Black political thought and ask the hard questions of themselves and us.

Grateful acknowledgment and special thanks to:

Gerald Shaka, bookstore owner/activist extraordinaire. His advice, "write what you know," led me to this book.

Marie Brown, my agent, for believing in this project from the start and translating its significance to my publisher. Her unwavering patience throughout the publication process was a constant reminder of the human side of this business of books.

Haki Madhubuti. His commitment to, passion for, and criticism of his own generation was in many ways the impetus for my inquiry into my own.

Sonia Sanchez. Our conversations about the contradictions of her generation's activists and intellectuals, especially when it comes to the gender divide, encouraged me to think deeper about the war of the sexes in the hip-hop generation.

David Mays, Carlito Rodriguez, Jeremy Miller, Alan Gordon, Ron Horton, and all my peeps at *The Source*. The many intra-office debates about hip-hop in general, especially the place of various cultures, ethnic groups, and races in it, as well as the fierce arguments over which social and political issues were relevant to the "average kid on the street," helped focus this book.

Sarah McNally, my editor. Her contemplative questions, gentle but firm prodding, and brilliant sense of structure made this book infinitely more compelling than the original manuscript.

INTRODUCTION

Confronting the Crises in African American Culture

> BACK 'N THE DAY OUR PARENTS USED TO TAKE
>   CARE OF US
> LOOK AT 'EM NOW, THEY EVEN FUCKIN' SCARED OF US
> CALLIN' THE CITY FOR HELP BECAUSE THEY CAN'T
>   MAINTAIN
> DAMN SHIT DONE CHANGED.
> —NOTORIOUS B.I.G., "THINGS DONE CHANGED"

THE MORNING FOLLOWING THE 2000 PRESIDENTIAL ELECTION, I received a call from a fifty-year-old Italian American friend, a former '60s Berkeley radical, lamenting how devastating an almost certain George W. Bush win would be for young African Americans. His sentiments echoed those of a handful of young Black students at a small, Midwest liberal arts college whom I had met with the night before to discuss the election, hip-hop generation voter participation, and ways of moving the hip-hop generation into the mainstream political process. "It must be a really sad day to be young and Black in America," he told me somewhat apologetically.

As I contemplate the unique challenges facing our generation of African American youth, those words reverberate in my thoughts. Although he was referring to disenfranchisement and a growing American conservatism, for the students, like most hip-hop generationers, a George W. win, in the final analysis, pales in comparison to the field of crises already afoot in African American culture, crises that threaten the very future of African American life.

These crises are interconnected, bound by the cross-section of racial politics, shifts in the American economy over the past two decades, and significant changes in Black youth culture. Leading the list is America's unfulfilled promise of equality and inclusion. Great disparities in education, housing, health care, employment opportunities, wages, mortgage loan approval, and the like persist. Collectively, these disparities have profoundly impacted our generation, though we have lived our entire lives in post-segregation America. Part of the promise, most certainly, following the civil rights movement was that these problems would be eradicated. The many side effects of the ever-looming war on drugs, the escalating tensions between young Black men and women, and the great intergenerational abyss, dubbed the generation gap, pose an array of previously unseen challenges in African American life.

Despite their magnitude, these issues, particularly as they affect hip-hop generationers, get lost in contemporary popular discussion, media reports, and public policy. One reason for this is that African American youth, for much of the past two decades, have been deemed the problem—whether criminalized in sensational news crime reports or demonized as the architects of America's declining moral values. Another reason is the near obsessive national attention given to praising the long gone civil rights movement. Ignored is the grim reality that concrete progress within the civil rights arena has been almost nil for nearly four decades. Neither acknowledged are the ways persisting institutionalized racism has intensified for hip-hop generationers despite 1950s and 1960s civil rights legislation.

A final obstacle is the unprecedented influence Black youth have achieved through popular culture, especially via the hip-hop phenomenon. Young Blacks have used this access, both in pop film and music, far too much to strengthen associations between Blackness and poverty, while celebrating anti-intellectualism, ignorance, irresponsible parenthood, and criminal lifestyles. This is the paradox: given hip-hop's growing influence, these *Birth of a Nation*–styled representations receive a free pass from Black leaders and organizations seeking influence with the younger generation. These depictions also escape any real criticism from non-Black critics who, having grown tired of the race card, fear being attacked as racist. Void of open and consistent criticism, such widely distributed incendiary ideas (what cultural critic Stanley Crouch calls "the new minstrelsy") reinforce myths of Black inferiority and insulate the new problems in African American culture from redemptive criticism.

What is to be done? The necessary first step toward illuminating and addressing the new crises in African American life is to understand the generation most heavily besieged by them. Those genuinely concerned about these crises must begin to carefully examine the major social and political forces shaping young Black Americans at the dawn of the twenty-first century. Rather than be shortchanged by worn ways of thinking about Black life, this criticism must be bold, unapologetic, painstaking, and unbound by traditional political orientations.

This criticism must use a clear lens to examine, at the very minimum, the following questions. How is the worldview of the generation of young Blacks born between 1965 and 1984 different from those of previous generations? How have high incarceration rates affected our lives? What issues are the focal points for this generation's activism and political agenda? Why do unemployment rates of young Blacks remain twice those of their white counterparts? What distinguishes this generation's war of the sexes from that of our parents? What does it mean to be the first generation of African Americans to come of age in post-segregation America? How has coming of age amidst an emerging global economy influenced our worldview? These questions—the answers to which begin to explain this generation's career choices, relationships, education, music, politics, activism, and lifestyle—probe the roots of the crises that now threaten to envelop us.

The examination of the hip-hop generation that follows is an attempt to jump-start the dialogue necessary to change our current course. The *Fire Next Time* that James Baldwin predicted in 1963 is upon us. And what we are seeing, as quiet as it's kept, is only a glimpse of what awaits us. Although conditions facing young Blacks in today's America are cause for concern and, yes, sadness, there is much hope and great possibility if we now, before it is too late, together, Americans old and young, across race and gender, with criticism, insight and concern, rise to the challenge.

Part ONE

THE NEW CRISES IN AFRICAN AMERICAN CULTURE

1

THE NEW BLACK YOUTH CULTURE

The Emergence of the Hip-Hop Generation

I'VE HEARD ENOUGH OF [OUR YOUTH] TO KNOW THAT WE OUGHT TO BE HOLDING THEM UP AND SHARING WITH THEM WHAT WE KNOW INSTEAD OF STANDING ON TOP OF THEM TELLING THEM WHAT THEY'RE NOT DOING RIGHT. THEY'RE DOING A LOT RIGHT AND SOME THINGS WRONG. WE CONTINUE TO FAIL THESE BRILLIANT, VERY TALENTED, VERY CREATIVE AND COURAGEOUS YOUNG PEOPLE BECAUSE THEY'RE NOT SAYING WHAT OUR MESSAGE WAS. BUT FOR CHRIST'S SAKE . . . WE'RE ABOUT TO ENTER THE 21ST CENTURY. SOMETHING SHOULD BE DIFFERENT. AND THEY MAY BE RIGHT ABOUT SOME THINGS.

—AFENI SHAKUR, FORMER BLACK PANTHER,
MOTHER OF RAPPER TUPAC SHAKUR

ASK ANY YOUNG BLACK AMERICAN BORN BETWEEN 1965 AND 1984 where they were on September 13, 1996, and most can

3

tell you. Ask them where they were six months later on March 9, 1997, and you'll get recollections as crystal clear as a baby boomer reminiscing on his or her whereabouts upon hearing of the assassinations of President Kennedy, Martin Luther King Jr., or Malcolm X. The September 1996 death of twenty-five-year-old Tupac Shakur was followed by memorials in New York City, Los Angeles, and several cities in between. Likewise the March 1997 death of Christopher Wallace, aka Notorious B.I.G., did not pass without the recognition of his peers. The twenty-four-year-old was commemorated with a statesman-like funeral procession through his old stomping grounds. The deaths of both rap artists fueled record sales of their CDs. Their music and their lives became the subjects of books, college courses, television documentaries, and conference discussions. Killed in a hail of bullets fired by unknown gunmen, both rappers were deemed by countless critics as irresponsible, self-centered thugs who sowed the seeds of their own destruction. Those fans who celebrated their lives were seen as equally irresponsible. But the outpouring of affection was more than simply a fascination with the underworld of rap music and its entertainers. This commemoration of B.I.G. and Pac marked a turning point. Not only had we, the hip-hop generation, come of age, but more importantly, we were conscious of our arrival.

Both rappers, like their peers who saw hope and promise in their short lives, were hip-hop generationers—those young African Americans born between 1965 and 1984 who came of age in the eighties and nineties and who share a specific set of values and attitudes. At the core are our thoughts about family, relationships, child rearing, career, racial identity, race relations, and politics. Collectively, these views make up a complex worldview that has not been concretely defined.

This worldview first began to be expressed in the insightful mid- to late 1980s sociopolitical critiques of rap artists like NWA, KRS-One, Poor Righteous Teachers, Queen Latifah, and others. In the mid-1990s, a handful of young writers such as Carlito Rodriguez, Bonz Malone, Selwyn Hinds, Mimi Valdez, and Scoop Jackson, to name a few, captured this sensibility in their work—although their essays were marginalized in magazines like *The Source, Vibe,* and *Rap Pages.* Filmmakers like John Singleton, Albert and Allen Hughes, and Hype Williams (particularly in their 1990s films *Boyz N the Hood, Menace II Society,* and *Belly,* respectively), also deftly presented these nuances—as do the youth-specific political concerns articulated almost daily by young activists like Conrad Muhammad, Lisa Sullivan, DeLacy Davis, and Donna Frisby-Greenwood.[1] A delayed response has more recently come out of the academy, most notably in the work of young scholars like historian Robin Kelley and sociologist Mary Pattillo-McCoy.

Collectively, hip-hop-generation writers, artists, filmmakers, activists, and scholars like these laid the foundation for understanding our generation's worldview. Mary Pattillo-McCoy's *Black Picket Fences: Privilege and Peril Among the Black Middle Class* (University of Chicago, 1999), in comparing middle-class Black Americans to their white counterparts, put it this way:

> We know that middle-class African Americans do not perform as well as whites on standardized tests (in school or in employment); are more likely to be incarcerated for drug offenses; are less likely to marry and

---

[1]Conrad Muhammad, executive director of A Movement for CHHANGE; Lisa Sullivan, executive director of Local Initiative, Support, Training, and Education Network, Incorporated (LISTEN, Inc.); DeLacy Davis, president of Black Cops Against Police Brutality; Donna Frisby-Greenwood, executive director of Inner City Games.

more likely to have a child without being married; and are less likely to be working.

Pattillo-McCoy makes clear that even though this Black middle class is about half of the Black population, almost half of it is concentrated in the lower-middle-class region. Pattillo-McCoy also states that this Black middle class is distinguished by its close proximity to the Black working poor. I would add that what Pattillo-McCoy describes above extends to poor and working-class Blacks and not just in comparison to their white counterparts but, more importantly, relative to our parents' generation as well. In reaching these conclusions, Pattillo-McCoy relies on the objective evidence, but this worldview also extends to what we believe.

Of course, this definition is still fluid as this generation continues to come into its own. But I would further generalize that we, like our white peers, are more likely than our parents' generation to be obsessed with our careers and getting rich quick. For us, achieving wealth, by any means necessary, is more important than most anything else, hence our obsession with the materialistic and consumer trappings of financial success. Central to our identity is a severe sense of alienation between the sexes. Likewise, our perspective on personal relationships and marriage is more likely to take into consideration concerns as diverse as our parents' generation's divorce rates and child support enforcement laws, and we are more likely to be open to family arrangements other than the traditional American family. At the same time, our views of politics, race relations, and racial identity are more likely to have been shaped by Jesse Jackson's 1984 and 1988 presidential campaigns, the 1992 Los Angeles riots, and/or the Million Man March. Our views about safe sex are more likely to have been influenced by Easy E or Magic Johnson's public announcements regarding themselves and HIV/AIDS.

That Black youth share a national culture is nothing new in itself. Black youth culture during the 1920s, the 1930s, and even the 1960s was national in scope. Yet, during each of these periods, Black youth were more likely to derive values and identity from such traditional community institutions as family, church, and school. Despite slight local variations, the passing on of Black culture to the succeeding generation remained orderly and consistent from one Black community to the next. Today the influence of these traditional purveyors of Black culture have largely diminished in the face of powerful and pervasive technological advances and corporate growth. Now media and entertainment such as pop music, film, and fashion are among the major forces transmitting culture to this generation of Black Americans. At the same time, the new Black youth culture cuts across class lines, so that whether one is middle class, coming of age in a suburban or rural setting, college-bound, or a street-wise urban dweller, what it means to be young and Black has been similarly redefined. As such, the defining values of this generation's worldview have taken a dramatic turn away from our parents' generation.

For our parent's generation, the political ideals of civil rights and Black power are central to their worldview. Our parent's generation placed family, spirituality, social responsibility, and Black pride at the center of their identity as Black Americans. They, like their parents before them, looked to their elders for values and identity. The core set of values shared by a large segment of the hip-hop generation—Black America's generation X—stands in contrast to our parents' worldview. For the most part, we have turned to ourselves, our peers, global images and products, and the new realities we face for guidance. In the process, the values and attitudes described above anchor our worldview.

Our parents' values maintain a strong presence within our worldview. But in cases where the old and the new collide, the old—more often than not—is superseded by the new. For example, Black pride is still an important part of this generation's identity. In fact, the hip-hop generation has embraced the idea of Blackness in ways that parallel the Black consciousness raising of the late 1960s and early 1970s. The popularization of the Afrocentric movement from the late 1980s through the 1990s, pro-Black lyrics on the contemporary rap scene, as well as traditional hairstyles (dreadlocks and braids, for example) adopted by many hip-hop generationers all speak to this. Regardless of whether this is a brand of hard-core nationalism or a lukewarm, flash-in-the-pan bou-gie nationalism, the fact remains that when many hip-hop generation youth have to choose between personal financial success at the expense of what the older generation considers communal cultural integrity, individual gain generally comes first.

It is important to distinguish this worldview from hip-hop culture, the youth-oriented lifestyle that birthed rap music. Certainly, the commercialization of rap music expanded the definition of hip-hop culture beyond the four elements (graffiti, break dancing, dj-ing, rap music) to include verbal language, body language, attitude, style, and fashion. By contrast, the new Black youth culture is expressed both publicly and privately in myriad ways. You see the street culture manifestation of this in "'hood" films and hip-hop magazines like *The Source* as much as in rap music and hip-hop culture. You see it in the defiant attitude and disposition of our generation's professional athletes and entertainers like Allen Iverson, Ray Lewis, Mike Tyson, Randy Moss, and Albert Bell. You see it in the activism of the younger generation, which not only fights the power coming from the mainstream politics but is routinely at odds with older-generation activists like Jesse Jackson, Kweisi Mfume, and Al Sharpton. You see it coming from happy-to-be-middle-class-themed magazines like *Honey* and *Savoy* as well as like-minded, youth-oriented television programming such as MTV and on-line publications like BET.com.

What were the catalysts for this new worldview? Like any generation, much of the hip-hop generation's group identity has been shaped by the major sociopolitical forces of our formative years. At least six major phenomena that emerged in the 1980s and 1990s have had a major impact on this generation's way of viewing the world.

Let us begin with popular culture and the visibility of Black youth within it. Today, more and more Black youth are turning to rap music, music videos, designer clothing, popular Black films, and television programs for values and identity. One can find the faces, bodies, attitudes, and language of Black youth attached to slick advertisements that sell what have become global products, whether it's Coca-Cola and Pepsi, Reebok and Nike sneakers, films such as *Love Jones* and *Set It Off*, or popular rap artists like Missy Elliot and Busta Rhymes. Working diligently behind the scene and toward the bottom line are the multinational corporations that produce, distribute, and shape these images. That Black youth in New Orleans, Louisiana, and Champaign, Illinois, for example, share similar dress styles, colloquialisms, and body language with urban kids from Los Angeles, Chicago, and New York City is not coincidental.

We live in an age where corporate mergers, particularly in media and entertainment, have redefined public space. Within this largely expanded public space, the viewing public is constantly bombarded by visual images that have become central to the identity of an entire generation. Within the arena of popular culture, rap music more than anything else has helped shape the new Black youth culture. From 1997 to 1998, rap music sales showed a 31 percent increase, making rap the fastest growing music genre, ahead of country, rock, classical, and all other musical forms. By 1998 rap was the top-selling musical format, outdistancing rock music and country music, the previous leading sellers. Rap music's prominence on the American music scene was evident by the late 1990s—from its increasing presence at the Grammy's (which in 1998, for example, awarded rapper Lauryn Hill five awards) to its pervasiveness in advertisements for mainstream corporations like AT&T, The Gap, Levi's, and so on.

Cultural critic Cornel West, in his prophetic *Race Matters* (Beacon Press, 1993), refers to this high level of visibility of young Blacks, primarily professional athletes and entertainers, in American popular culture as the Afro-Americanization of white youth.

> The Afro-Americanization of white youth has been more a male than female affair given the prominence of male athletes and the cultural weight of male pop artists. This process results in white youth—male and female—imitating and emulating black male styles of walking, talking, dressing and gesticulating in relations to others. The irony in our present moment is that just as young black men are murdered, maimed and imprisoned in record numbers, their styles have become disproportionately influential in shaping popular culture.

Whereas previously the voices of young Blacks had been locked out of the global age's public square, the mainstreaming of rap music now gave Black youth more visibility and a broader platform than we had ever enjoyed before. At the same time, it gave young Blacks across the country who identified with it and were informed by it a medium through which to share a national culture. In the process, rap artists became the dominant public voice of this generation. Many have been effective in bringing the generation's issues to the fore. From NWA to Master P, rappers—through their lyrics, style, and attitude—helped to carve a new Black youth identity into the national landscape. Rappers' access to global media and their use of popular culture to articulate many aspects of this national identity renders rap music central to any discussion of the new Black youth culture. The irony in all this is that the global corporate structure that gave young Blacks a platform was the driving force behind our plight.

In fact, the face of globalization that emerged in the 1980s and 1990s is itself a critical factor that has significantly influenced the worldview of hip-hop generationers. In short, the transnational corporations of the 1970s evolved into the mega-corporations of the 1980s, 1990s, and beyond. Several hundred of these giants, some with economies larger than most countries, collectively make up what is commonly referred to as the global economy—although there are now literally tens of thousands of smaller corporations operating at a global level, based primarily in the United States, Japan, and Europe. These mega-corporations are fueled by cutting-edge biological and digital technology and are impacting the lives of most of the world's population through their integration of commerce. As everyday people worldwide struggle to survive, these corporations work diligently to sell them a slice of modern life—from automobiles and electronics to food and entertainment. Global corporations—with the help of global institutions like the World Bank, the World Trade Organization, and the International Monetary Fund—have created immense wealth, further concentrated it in the hands of a few, and escalated the widening division between the haves and the have-nots. These mega-corporations are enabled by international trade agreements like NAFTA (North America Free Trade Agreement) and GATT (General Agreement on Tariffs and Trade). This reorganization of the world economy has filtered down to the lives of everyday people, including African Americans, in ways that are highly contradictory.

Young Black Americans born between 1965 and 1984 are the first generation of Black Americans to come of age in the era of globalization. Globalization certainly accounts for some "positive" outcomes, such as the success of rap music described above. In terms of wealth, those hip-hop generationers who are at the upper end of the middle class and beyond have enjoyed increased income and wealth during the 1980s and 1990s. Increases in income among college-educated professionals account for some of this; professional athletes and entertainers as well as a small number of young Blacks who cashed in on the high-tech boom of the 1990s account for much more. It must be emphasized that these individuals constitute a very small elite.

The real story of globalization's impact on the hip-hop generation is revealed in the widening division between the haves and have-nots that occurred during the 1980s and 1990s. Richard Freeman and Lawrence Katz, editors of *Differences and Changes in Wage Structures* (University of Chicago, 1995) investigated this trend and concluded:

> Earnings inequality increased substantially in the United States in the 1980s, and the real earnings of many groups of workers, primarily men, fell from the early 1970s through the early 1990s. . . . In short, in the 1980s, if not earlier, the U.S. labor market experienced a massive twist against the less skilled and lower paid that reduced their living standards.

Experts like these point to movement of manufacturing jobs away from urban centers to the suburbs and overseas as a major factor in wage stagnation from the early to mid-1970s through the 1980s and into the 1990s. Before this period, the Black middle class had been steadily growing since World War II. Despite the celebration of "the new Black middle class" in sensational media reports and self-congratulatory books like Lawrence Otis Graham's *Our Kind of People* and Ellis Cose's *The Rage of a Privileged Class*, no subsequent real growth of the Black middle class occurred until the very end of the 1990s, when Black poverty rates began to decline for the first time in more than twenty years. During the intervening period of the 1980s and 1990s, young Blacks faced the realities of rising rates of unemployment, Black youth reliance on the underground economy, particularly the crack-cocaine explosion of the 1980s, and the simultaneous boom in incarceration rates. The great contrast between the positive and negative outgrowths of this new global economy has heavily influenced the values, lifestyles, and worldview of young Blacks.

Third, the worldview of hip-hop generationers has been influenced by persisting segregation in an America that preaches democracy and inclusion. This contradiction has been particularly hard for us to swallow. Our generation is the first generation of African Americans to come of age outside the confines of legal segregation. We certainly live in a more inclusive society than existed in pre–civil rights America. However, continuing segregation and inequality have made it especially illusory for many young Blacks. The illusion of integration allows for some access, while countless roadblocks persist in critical areas where Blacks continue to be discriminated against in often subtle and sometimes not so subtle ways. Young Blacks are twice as likely to be unemployed as their white counterparts. Young Blacks with similar skills, experience, and educational backgrounds continue to be paid less than whites for the same jobs. More so than any other racial or ethnic group, African Americans remain segregated from whites in housing. In terms of electoral politics, although there are more Black elected officials than ever before (nearly 9,000 in 1999, according to the Joint Center for Political and Economic Studies), Black politicians find it nearly impossible to get elected to statewide office in majority white states. In nearly forty years, only two Blacks have been elected to the U.S. Senate, and only one Black has been elected governor of any state. These obstacles in the face of lip service to human rights and democracy foster resentment among young Blacks. Inevitably, the contradictions of these racial double standards are embedded in our worldview.

A fourth impact on our worldview has been public policy regarding criminal justice, particularly policy that has clear racial implications. Beginning as early as 1982, such national policy was highlighted by initiatives such as the Reagan administration's "War on Drugs," which relaunched earlier anti-drug efforts by heavily shifting the focus of fighting illegal drug use from rehabilitation to punishment. The Omnibus Crime Bill of 1984, the 1986 Anti-Drug Abuse Act, and the 1988 Omnibus Anti-Drug Abuse Act were all part of the 1980s wave of legislation aimed at getting tough on crime. The most controversial aspects of these laws were elements like the disparity in sentencing for crack cocaine and powder cocaine. Offenders convicted of crimes involving as little as five grams of crack cocaine receive a minimum of five years in prison. For a powder cocaine offender to receive a similar sentence, the crime would have to involve nearly one hundred times that amount. Critics charge that the disparity is unjustified as there is no chemical difference between the two. The only difference is that the low cost of crack makes it affordable to almost anyone. According to the National Institute on Drug Abuse, by 1990 most crack cocaine users were white. Yet, in the early 1990s, 90 percent of those convicted in federal court of crack cocaine crimes were Black.

In a similar vein, in 1992 the Bush administration created the Violence Initiative, a series of federally funded studies that sought behavioral and biological markers for predicting a propensity for violence in young males. Under the auspices of helping "at least 100,000 inner-city kids," the studies also developed intervention models. Although the name Violence Initiative was dropped following protests from civil rights groups who claimed the studies attempted to determine that young Blacks were biologically prone to violence, the government continues to spend at least $50 million annually on such studies.

These efforts dovetailed into the Clinton administration's Violent Crime Control and Law Enforcement Act of 1994, a $30 billion appropriation that earmarked nearly $10 billion for prison construction alone and sanctioned the death penalty for federal crimes commonly associated with inner-city young Blacks and Latinos, such as carjacking and drive-by shootings. The law also targeted gang members with new and harsher penalties for drug crimes, and made life imprisonment mandatory for federal offenders after more than two state or federal convictions for violent felonies or drug crimes (three strikes). Finally, the 1994 law called for adult prosecution of thirteen- and fourteen-year-olds charged with certain violent crimes. Some lawmakers went even further in turning up the heat on young violent offenders. This was especially true of the Juvenile Crime Control Act, a bill that received tons of media coverage but never made it into federal law. However, between 1992 and 1997, all but six states adopted its main tenants, which allowed youths to be tried as adults, allocated funds for more prison construction, and relaxed laws that restricted the housing of youths in adult facilities.

In addition to federal legislation, local laws that criminalized Black youth behavior were a mainstay of the 1990s as well. In 1992, for example, Chicago lawmakers enacted an anti-gang loitering ordinance. Following in the footsteps of other cities whose anti-drug/anti-gang efforts quickly collapsed into anti-youth laws, Chicago's ordinance prohibited two or more youth from loitering in public places like the sidewalk in front of their homes, the neighborhood park, and so forth. Convictions carried a maximum six-month prison sentence and $500 fine. The idea was to keep gang members off the streets and thereby stop crimes before they occurred. However, Chicago's anti-gang loitering ordinance went one step further. Police were given the authority to order loiterers to move on if they suspected that one was a gang member. Nearly 40,000 youth were arrested under the law within a two-year period. In 1999, the Supreme Court ruled that the law was unconstitutional, but such legislation persists.

Furthermore, various styles of dress, hairstyles, and fashion popular among Black youth have been banned from many of the nation's schools and in some communities make one subject to arrest. In the mid- to late 1990s, law enforcement agencies in Chicago, Houston, and Los Angeles, as well as countless smaller cities, began to develop "gang profiling" databases. These databases consist of suspected gang members and their family, friends, and associates. Some include photographs and other categorized data that can be used against individuals in court. Most of those found in these databases are young Blacks and Latinos, as some of the characteristics used in profiling include being a member of a racial minority, graffiti writing, and dressing in a particular manner. In Los Angeles, the sheriff's department stores information on at least 140,000 individuals, many of whom have not committed any crime. Across the country, policies like these have became common in the 1990s.

This legislative association of Black youth with criminality inevitably spills over into law enforcement. Throughout the decade between the Rodney King beating in 1991 and the police shooting death of Timothy Thomas, nineteen, in Cincinnati in 2001, incidents of brutality and murder—often deemed justifiable homicide—have continued unabated. Christian Parenti in his illuminating *Lockdown America: Police and Prisons in the Age of Crisis* (Verso, 1999) asserts that this is part of a 1980s and 1990s nationwide trend in policing designed to put the force back in the police industry.

> In the last decade the pressure to police effectively and secure urban space has become all the more important. For centuries, "the urban" has been synonymous with filth, lawlessness, and danger, but in recent years cities have also taken on a renewed economic and cultural importance as sites of accumulation, speculation, and innovative profit making. For cities to work as such, they must be, or at least appear and feel, safe. If the economic restructuring of the eighties and nineties intensified urban poverty, it also created new, gilded spaces that are increasingly *threatened by poverty*. This polarization of urban space and social relations has in turn required a new layer of regulation and exclusion, so as to protect the new hyper-aestheticized, playground quarters of the postmodern metropolis from their flipsides of misery. This contradiction, between the danger of cities and their value, has spawned yet another revolution in American law enforcement: the rise of zero-tolerance/quality of life policing.

Parenti says this style of policing has naturally led to rising rates of police brutality, especially against people of color. In New York City, complaints of police brutality rose nearly 50 percent in 1994 alone, according to Parenti.

This seemingly open season on young Blacks by police officers is a pattern that too often has repeated itself throughout the 1980s and 1990s. The mass demonstrations, including those that followed the Rodney King beating in Los Angeles, Malice Green's murder in Detroit, Johnny Gammage's murder by police in Pittsburgh, Abner Louima's beating in New York City, and Amadou Diallo's murder by officers in New York City, reflect overwhelming frustration and a growing cynicism about policing that has reached an all time high. This collapse of trust in law enforcement and the vilification of Black youth through crime legislation certainly play a role in the view Black youth share about legislation, law enforcement, and criminal justice.

Fifth in our discussion of influences on the new Black youth culture is the media representation of young Blacks. Prior to the 1990s mainstreaming of rap music, the nightly news was where young Blacks were most widely represented in terms of televised images. This media representation, as Mike Gray reveals in his *Drug Crazy: How We Got into This Mess and How We Can Get Out*, was critical to selling America on the war on drugs.

> The media in the 1980s got hooked on the drug war itself. . . . A surveillance van with a hidden camera can park on a street in Harlem, but it has no access to the Chicago Yacht Club or the ladies' room at Dan Tana's in West Hollywood. As a result, the drug-war footage showing up as the nightly news focused almost exclusively on the urban street scene, and though the vast majority of drug users have always been white, the people doing drugs on TV were now black and Hispanic. When a couple of researchers from the University of Michigan spotted this phenomenon . . . [they] discovered that from 1985 onward, the number of

whites shown using cocaine dropped by 60 percent, and the number of Blacks rose by the same amount.

This image of young Blacks persisted into the 1990s, although it was more and more counterbalanced by the visibility of young black professional athletes and entertainers.

Degrees of monstrousness of their crimes aside, the Lake Worth, Florida, Black thirteen-year-old Nathaniel Brazill, who shot and killed his English teacher, thirty-five-year-old Barry Grunow, became the poster boy for the turn-of-the-century spate of high school shootings rather than Dylan Klebold, seventeen, and Eric Harris, eighteen, who planned and carried out mass killings at Columbine High School in Littleton, Colorado, in 1999. Klebold and Harris killed twelve students and one teacher and injured nearly two dozen others before killing themselves. Likewise, Charles Andrew Williams, fifteen, opened fire on classmates at Santana High School in Santee, California, in March 2001, leaving two students dead and thirteen wounded.

Despite the cold-hearted, calculated nature of these white executioners, media coverage mainly humanized them. Commentary like this one from Nancy Gibbs writing in *Time* magazine (March 19, 2001) was the rule rather than the exception. "Given the agony that Williams inflicted on his victims," Gibbs wrote, "it is awkward even to discuss the agony that Williams was in." Yet Gibbs proceeded to do so, pointing the finger at the community and suburban culture as the cause of the crime rather than Williams himself.

> Some friends came to his defense, talked about how badly he had been treated, how the bullies stole his skateboard, stole even the shoes off his feet. Was there, this time, a measure of pity for a lost boy, who seemed to have had nowhere to go, who wore a silver necklace

with the word MOUSE on it, who called at least three
of his friends' mothers Mom, who in the end seemed to
want nothing more than to be taken seriously and to be
taken, at least, into somebody's custody?

Young Blacks who commit crimes, such as Brazill, rarely receive this kind of humanizing treatment in the mainstream
press. This contributes to the alienation of young Blacks
from the mainstream culture.

Finally, this generation's worldview has been affected by
the overall shift in the quality of life for young Blacks during
the 1980s and 1990s. Although by 1999, according to the U.S.
Census Bureau, the number of Blacks living below the
poverty line had dropped to its lowest level in nearly three
decades, many young Blacks remain poor and working
poor. The Urban Institute estimates that 60 percent of America's poor youth are Black. In addition, although unemployment rates for young Blacks had dropped by the late 1990s,
Black youth unemployment rates remain twice as high as
white youth unemployment rates (just as they have been for
the past two decades).

The rate of unemployment directly corresponds with the
number of youth involved in the underground economy.
The growth of youth street gangs, which experts say form
primarily to sell drugs, was a product of the 1980s and 1990s.
In 1995, the National Youth Gang Center of the Office of Juvenile Justice reported that gang activity existed in all fifty
states, including rural, urban, and suburban communities,
some but not all of which were Black. This underground
economy has contributed to the exorbitant number of Blacks
within the juvenile and adult criminal justice systems, which
by 1995 involved one-third of Black men between the ages of
eighteen and thirty-five, while juvenile arrests for females increased by 55 percent.

Statistics regarding gun homicide, suicide, and AIDS among young Blacks in the 1980s and 1990s provide a clear picture of the state of the hip-hop generation. Gun homicide has been the leading cause of death of Black men between the ages of fifteen and thirty-four since 1969. Today, like thirty years ago, young Black men are most likely to die at the hands of another young Black male. For Black males between the ages of eighteen and twenty-four, gun homicide increased 79 percent between 1980 and 1990.

Once nearly nonexistent among young Blacks, suicide, according to the Centers for Disease Control, is now the third leading cause of death for Blacks fifteen to twenty-four years old, the same as for the general population. The suicide rate for Black youth fifteen to nineteen years old more than doubled between 1980 and 1995, increasing most dramatically (146 percent) for young Black males ages 15–19. Nearly three-fourths of Black male teens who committed suicide in this period used guns to kill themselves.

And finally, AIDS, once a disease that struck primarily gay white men, fast became a disease of young Black heterosexuals during the 1990s. Compared to other racial and ethnic groups, Blacks have the highest rate of HIV infection in terms of new AIDS cases. But the situation is even more dire for young Blacks. According to the Centers for Disease Control, African American teens represent 60 percent of new AIDS cases among those aged 13–19. By 1999, according to the Department of Health and Human Services, AIDS was the leading cause of death among Black men ages 25–44 and the second leading cause of death for Black women in the same age group.

Why has the response to these monumental problems been so limited? When it comes to public policy and issues specific to Black youth, little happens beyond identifying the problems and discussing them. A large part of what stands in the way of implementing workable solutions is the steadily intensifying war going on inside Black America itself. The divide between the hip-hop generation and that of our parents (the civil rights/Black power generation) has not yet registered on the radar screen of cultural critics, activists, or policy makers. It is a divide that is as vast as the one that separated white America in the 1960s, as radical white youth culture broke from the mainstream and swept across the country.

When many of our parents, grandparents, and civil rights leaders disapprovingly comment on events like Freaknik (the annual gathering of Black college students in Atlanta), which over the years has devolved into a blend of general mayhem, partying, and in some cases incidents of violence, they are quick to recall earlier times in Black America when such behavior was not simply embarrassing to one's self and family but detrimental to the race overall. They point to this as evidence of how the hip-hop generation has veered off course.

A further indication of what they deem a withering sense of values and social responsibility among the younger generation, they say, is the steady drop in youth membership and attendance in the Black church—long a community haven of spiritual centeredness and respectable values. According to the National Opinion Research Center at the University of Chicago, attendance for eighteen to thirty-five-year-olds has dropped 5.6 percent from 1995 to 2000. (Black America's young energetic Christians like platinum-selling gospel singer Kirk Franklin are the exception rather than the rule.)

Likewise, it is not uncommon to hear some of these community leaders dismiss rap music—the most significant cultural achievement of our generation—as ghetto culture. Most of our parents, and especially civil rights leaders and community activists, would rather ignore rap's impact—especially those lyrics that delve into the gritty, street culture of the Black underworld—than explore its role in the lives of hip-hop generationers. At the core of each of these complaints is the voice of Black middle-class elitism. Another component of this criticism is fear—fear of what the older generation did to make the hip-hop generation so vastly different from their own. Another part of this criticism is rooted in the unwillingness among the older generation to adjust to the social transformations that have shaped the hip-hop generation.

"Each generation," writes Frantz Fanon in *The Wretched of the Earth*—the bible for activists in our parents' generation and a source often cited in the nostalgic search for deeper values within our own—"out of relative obscurity, must discover their mission, fulfill it or betray it." Now more than ever these divided generations must begin to understand the ways that the new Black youth culture both empowers and undermines Black America. As brilliant a moment in history as the civil rights and Black power eras were, the older generation must realize they cannot claim any real victory if the hip-hop generation cannot build significantly on those gains. The younger generation must understand that no matter how grand our individual achievements (achievements built on the gains from past struggles), they mean very little if we cannot overcome at least some of the major social obstacles of our time, leaving a formidable foundation on which the next generation can stand strong. As long as the older generation fails to understand the new Black youth culture in all of its complexities, and as long as the younger generation fails to see its inherent contradictions, we cannot as a community address the urgent crises now upon us, particularly those facing Black American youth. New ways of relieving current forms of oppression can be implemented only when the younger and older generations do so together. Our collective destiny demands it.

The rags-to-riches rap careers, the lyrics, and very lifestyles of Tupac and B.I.G. epitomize the new Black youth culture. Like their lives and deaths, each of these elements informs the worldview of our generation and speaks to our attitudes about all aspects of life from sex, love, and family to community, education, and future possibilities. This new Black youth culture raises some critical questions: how has Black America changed, what new circumstances and conditions have affected its evolution, and finally, what is the legacy of that culture at the dawn of the millennium? If Pac and B.I.G. are to be martyrs for the hip-hop generation, let them be martyrs in beginning an intergenerational movement to answer these questions and resolve those problems that threaten to undermine the very fabric and future of Black America.

2

AMERICA'S OUTCASTS

The Employment Crisis

IF I WASN'T IN THE RAP GAME,
I'D PROBABLY HAVE A KI KNEE-DEEP IN THE
    CRACK GAME.
CAUSE THE STREETS IS A SHORT STOP
EITHER YOU SLINGIN' CRACK ROCK OR YOU GOT A
    WICKED JUMP SHOT.
        —NOTORIOUS B.I.G., "THINGS DONE CHANGED"

ALTHOUGH OUR PARENTS' GENERATION FIRST SERIOUSLY
raised the issue of reparations in the 1970s (through activist-nationalist organizations like the Student Non-Violent Coordinating Committee [SNCC], the Republic of New Afrika, the National Coalition of Blacks for Reparations in America [N'COBRA], and religious-nationalist groups like the Nation of Islam), only in the past few years has the debate gained currency in the American mainstream.[1] Reparations, the idea

---

[1]Every year for the past twelve legislative sessions, Congressman John Conyers Jr. (D-Mich.), a baby boomer, has introduced a bill to establish a commission to explore the impact of slavery on African Americans and

that African Americans are owed compensation by the U.S. government and the corporations that benefited from the enslavement of our ancestors, is an issue that resonates with our generation, a significant segment of whom entered the job force in the 1980s and 1990s. As the first generation to come of age in post-segregation America, one would think that we, unlike previous generations, would have enjoyed a lifetime of social, economic, and political equality. Nothing could be further from the truth.

As the twentieth century came to a close, America experienced the largest economic expansion in its history. U.S. inflation and unemployment rates reached record lows. The stock market set one record high after another. Corporate profits continued to rise as computer technology increased efficiency across industries. All indicators suggested that the country's economy was sailing in the wind and that the good times, if not here for all, were at least bracing to trickle down on the horizon. But even before the economic meltdown at the dawn of new millennium, hip-hop generationers had little cause to celebrate. In fact, for the past two decades, Black rates of unemployment and unequal pay based on race have revealed that Blacks have been left out of America's thriving economy. A review of how we've fared in the labor market illustrates why the call for reparations strikes a chord with many hip-hop generationers almost to the point of common sense.

---

the feasibility of reparations—to no avail. His colleagues deem it a fruitless pursuit. The 2000 publication of *The Debt: What America Owes to Blacks*, by Randall Robinson, founder and president of TransAfrica, helped bring the discussion of reparations to the national spotlight. The pervasive countermovement to discredit the validity of reparations was exemplified by David Horowitz and his Center for the Study of Popular Culture's controversial "Ten Reasons Why Reparations for Blacks Is a Bad Idea—And Racist Too" advertisements, which ran in scores of college newspapers (including those at Brown University and U.C.–Berkeley) in the spring of 2001.

YOUNG BLACKS IN THE LABOR FORCE

The hip-hop generation, those Blacks born between 1965 and 1984, entered the job force during the 1980s and 1990s, a period marked by falling wages, worsening conditions for unskilled workers, and growing disparities in income and wealth between America's minority rich and majority poor. As the 1980s came to a close, the top 1 percent (834,000 households with a net worth of about $5.7 trillion) was worth more than the bottom 90 percent of Americans (94 million households with a net worth of $4.8 trillion) according to the Federal Reserve. The shift in wealth distribution was in part influenced by income, as the top 1 percent enjoyed the greatest gains in family income—70 percent from the late 1970s to the late 1980s. During the 1990s, the impact of the new global economy on the disparity in wealth was even more severe. By 1999, according to the Center on Budget and Policy Priorities, a Washington, D.C.–based think tank, the income gap between America's rich and poor reached a record high.

America's automated, service-oriented economy of the 1980s and 1990s witnessed a growing demand for highly skilled workers. Concurrently, the demand decreased for low-skilled workers who lacked the skills needed in the new economy. All the while, poverty increased. "For two decades, if not longer," report economists Richard Freeman and Peter Gottschalk in their 1998 book *Generating Jobs: How to Increase Demand for Less-Skilled Workers*, "the benefits of economic progress have been highly concentrated among the skilled and high-paid to the exclusion of many workers on the middle and lower rungs of the earnings distribution."

While it's true that globalization has negatively affected all low-skilled, working-class Americans, older workers have fared better than younger ones, and whites have fared better than Blacks. Thus the hip-hop generation has been hit particularly hard during these economic good times. At the dawn of the millennium, America's Black population is around 35 million or 13 percent of the U.S. population. Of the 35 million, approximately 9.5 million make up the hip-hop generation. In 1997, there were roughly 15.5 million Blacks in the labor force, of which nearly 14 million were employed. A college education remains the fastest route out of poverty, yet 83.7 percent of Blacks 25–64 years old in the labor force did not have a bachelor's degree. By comparison, 73.4 percent of whites lacked a bachelor's degree, and whites 25–34 years old tend to complete college at twice the rate of their Black peers. Of the 26.5 million whites 25–34 years old in the labor force, 31.9 percent (over 8 million) had at least a four-year college degree. By comparison, only 15.3 percent (less than 1 million) of the 5.3 million Blacks 25–34 years old had completed the same level of education.

Two characteristics distinguish our generation in the mainstream economy: (1) most are low-skilled workers, and (2) most are concentrated in urban communities with low job growth. U.S. Labor Department statistics show that 54.4 percent of all Blacks lived in urban centers in 1998 (compared to 22.5 percent of whites). With the trends of manufacturing jobs leaving the city and the suburbanization of employment well-entrenched by the 1980s, urban-dwelling young Blacks faced the worst employment prospects of all American workers. Despite limited government attempts to jump-start the economy in America's large cities and the success of some banks and businesses, few center cities have seen significant job growth.

Employment prospects for low-skilled Black workers were not always so bleak. In the 1950s and 1960s, many unskilled Black workers were employed in chemical, steel, rubber, auto, and meat-packing factories in northern cities during the Great Migration from the South. The freeze on immigration during the war years helped create a demand for Black low-skilled workers. Also, technological advances in the agricultural industry made many Black laborers in the South obsolete, opening up a potential labor pool. As center-city factory jobs drastically declined in the late 1960s and early 1970s, young low-skilled Black workers found work in government jobs, which resulted from new policy initiatives in the wake of the civil rights movement.

All that had changed by the 1980s, as companies pumped capital into automation and computerization in order to increase efficiency. Simultaneously, public policies that required government agencies to create jobs as a means of curbing unemployment (adopted by nearly every administration since the Great Depression) were abandoned.

By the 1980s, young Blacks who lacked the education demanded by these new high-tech jobs, especially workers concentrated in urban centers, had few places to go within the mainstream economy aside from minimum-wage jobs being created by the service sector. In 1997, the service sector produced more than 46 million jobs, 5.6 million of which went to Black workers.

Unlike the working-class jobs of the previous generation, however, most of these low-skilled jobs lack the wages and benefits that afforded low-skilled workers in the 1970s (postal and factory workers, for example) a middle-class existence. The previous generation's low-skilled workers could afford to buy homes and cars and had paid vacation time and other benefits. In contrast, the income earned by today's low-skilled young workers, especially in center cities, is inadequate for decent housing or child care. Most low-skilled young workers cannot afford apartments or homes; many live with their parents or relatives. Most are what social scientists call the "working poor," and their wages relegate them to a standard of living just above, at, or beneath the poverty line. In many cases, their parents enjoyed a higher standard of living.

THE MILITARY OPTION

Many hip-hop generationers have found the U.S. military to be one of the few realistic roads to economic stability. Whereas the previous generation was introduced to the armed forces primarily through the draft, this generation of military men has volunteered for military service. Of the 1.4 million active-duty men and women in all branches of the U.S. military, 275,000 are Black and 219,000 are hip-hop generationers. Of course, the size of the military has decreased considerably over the past decade by order of Congress (from 2.1 million in 1989), but Blacks continue to represent about 20 percent of the armed forces. Most are enlisted men.

Our generation's introduction to military service as an employment option came in the way of commercials with catchy slogans in the 1980s such as "Be all that you can be in the Army." (For our generation, everything, even military service, is commodified.) Many young Blacks joined the military because of limited employment options in our communities. With the end of the Cold War, it seemed that the armed services were destined for peaceful missions, so much so that the mystique of joining the military for many in our generation came to be synonymous with travel, adventure, and obtaining work skills (just as the Army ads portrayed), rather than engaging in combat.

Nevertheless, the hip-hop generation has seen its share of wars. Many young African American soldiers have served in one or more missions of the 1980s and 1990s, including the invasion of Grenada, the Persian Gulf War, and engagements in Somalia, Bosnia, and Kosovo. Inevitably, many of them struggle with the contradiction of fighting to secure democracy and free-market economics abroad, while they lack opportunities themselves at home and neglected Black communities in center cities remain likened to war zones. "I just can't stop thinking about how all of the money that will be spent on this operation could be put into our communities, doing stuff to better our situation," said Samuel Everett at the start of the U.S. military involvement in the peacekeeping mission in Bosnia in 1996, voicing a growing concern of hip-hop generationers who've enlisted in the military. "Everyone should know you gotta take care of home first."

At the start of the Bosnia peacekeeping mission, Everett was a corporal. Since then, he's been promoted to sergeant. At twenty-eight, he has spent the past decade of his life in the military. His life as a military man is similar to that of many Black soldiers of our generation. They share similar pay—entry-level pay is around $1,000 per month plus a housing allowance and bonuses—and benefits, such as health care and dental care. After completion of their first tour of duty, most are eligible for financial support for college attendance (more than $20,000 in the mid-1980s and up to $50,000 by 2000) and low-interest home loans. After twenty years of service, soldiers receive retirement pensions. Most see military service as a way out of a potentially troubled life of low-paying, low-skilled jobs or life in the underground economy, which is often accompanied by the very real threat of prison. Military service enables them to earn a regular paycheck, make a decent living, escape life in impoverished, jobless communities, move out of their parents' home, and earn the respect and honor of workers contributing to the good of society.

Everett's remark about not "taking care of home" echoes a sentiment common among many Black enlisted men and women in our generation. But the criticism within the ranks does not begin to match the growing cynicism of those outside. Given the field of options for most unskilled hip-hop generation workers, the army is the best show in town. Nevertheless, the benefits offered by the armed services are not enough to maintain in today's economy. This has led to a downturn in the number of Black youth looking to the military as an option. By 1999, after years of decline, army enlistment dropped to its lowest level since 1979. Experts point to a lack of interest in volunteerism among our generation and to the military's lack of clarity about its post–Cold War mission. However, the more plausible explanation (the absurdity of mercenary as your best job option in the world's most economically advanced culture, aside) relates to the difficulty soldiers have making ends meet.

Although military service compares somewhat favorably to other options available to young Black unskilled workers, the compensation for most enlistees is inadequate. Those with families often qualify for the federal WIC (Women, Infants, and Children) food program, to the extent that WIC offices are now located on several military bases. One navy fire controlman, who earns extra money delivering pizzas, told *USA Today* (March 18, 1999), "If you've got a family, you need to get a second job." Increasingly, soldiers are supplementing their income with additional jobs in the formal and informal economy—from working part-time, minimum-wage service industry jobs to joining drug-selling gangs. Although the army estimates that less than 1 percent of its soldiers join drug-selling gangs, even this small percentage highlights the dire employment situation facing our generation both in civilian and in military life.

GLOBAL ECONOMY AT HOME AND ABROAD

The term "global economy" has become one of today's catchwords. Though we commonly accept the reality of this new phenomenon, its most harmful effects are rarely discussed. Although its origins are subject to debate, few dispute the critical impact of the creation of the International Monetary Fund (IMF) and the World Bank in the mid-1940s. Under the guidance of these two institutions, free-market policies have been established around the globe, disrupting the local economies of weaker countries and opening them up to dependency on imports from mostly Western-based foreign multinationals. The results, more often than not, have been disastrous for workers.

Just as globalization has affected employment options for low-skilled workers at home (corporations closing U.S. factories, laying off workers, and "exporting" U.S. jobs to lower-wage workers abroad), it has also impacted workers worldwide. The coming of structural adjustment programs and multinational corporate factories to places like Indonesia, for example, has undermined previously agriculture-based local economies. In the 1970s, countless young people left farms and flocked to factory jobs (provided by multinational corporations) in urban areas like Jakarta. With the 1998 collapse of the economy in Southeast Asia, many of these workers lost their jobs and now have nowhere to turn. It is a pattern that is being repeated around the globe. In many cases, nearly three decades of global economic growth has translated into fewer jobs, a lower standard of living, and increased poverty.

The mid-1970s to the mid-1980s were critical years in establishing the new economy. During these years, the corporate practice of exporting low-skilled manufacturing jobs became commonplace. National unemployment rates, particularly Black youth unemployment rates, skyrocketed. In the preceding decade, the poverty rate had steadily declined from 30 percent in 1960 to 11.1 percent by 1973. The growth of multinational corporations in size, wealth, and power, the deregulation of international banking and financial markets (alongside technological advances that allowed investors to move large quantities of money from market to market), and a Federal Reserve, once concerned with achieving full employment, that shifted its focus to lowering inflation and slowing growth all contributed to the decline of union influence and the collective bargaining power of workers. This, in turn, has helped to create an international minimum wage and ushered in worsening conditions for workers worldwide.

With these economic shifts came automation, privatization, corporate mega-mergers, and downsizing—all steps along the road to globalization. At home, as the new economy marched forward, supportive politicians and economists insisted that what was good for American-based global corporations was good for the national economy and for American workers. Corporate profit, they argued, would trickle down to all workers. But the trickle-down never came. Instead hundreds of thousands of jobs were lost in the 1980s.

In rural areas like Appalachia's Inez, Kentucky, coal companies halved their local workforce, replacing miners with machines. And in urban centers like Los Angeles' South Central area, the shutdown of manufacturers like Goodyear Tire, General Motors, and Bethlehem Steel further escalated unemployment and sent many youth outside of the mainstream economy to make ends meet. Sociologist William Julius Wilson in his book *When Work Disappears: The World of the New Urban Poor* (Vintage Books, 1997) describes it this way:

> Neighborhoods that offer few legitimate employment opportunities, inadequate job information networks, and poor schools lead to the disappearance of work. That is, where jobs are scarce, where people rarely, if ever, have the opportunity to help their friends and neighbors find jobs, and where there is a disruptive or

degraded school life purporting to prepare youngsters for eventual participation in the workforce, many people eventually lose their feeling of connectedness to work in the formal economy; they no longer expect work to be a regular, and regulating, force in their lives. In the case of young people, they may grow up in an environment that lacks the idea of work as a central experience of adult life—they have little or no labor-force attachment. These circumstances also increase the likelihood that the residents will rely on illegitimate sources of income, thereby further weakening their attachment to the legitimate labor market.

In the 1980s and 1990s, many hip-hop generationers quickly realized that a forty-hour-a-week, minimum-wage job wouldn't meet their basic needs. That many of us would take our chances in the informal economy is not surprising, hence the mass appeal enjoyed by rap lyrics that described a gritty underworld. Young Black and Latino audiences identify with this message because it is familiar. Increasingly young whites and other American racial and ethnic groups living in pockets of poverty in suburban and rural communities are identifying with it for the same reason. The impact of globalization has not stopped at traditional borders. Although young Blacks suffer from the additional burden of racial discrimination, poor and middle-class young whites are not immune from the impacts of economic change, a fact highlighted by the continuing world trade protests.

SOCIAL PROTESTS OF THE 1980S AND 1990S

In 1970, Sidney Willhelm wrote in his prophetic *Who Needs the Negro* (Schenkman, 1970) that Black labor, something America had taken advantage of for more than 350 years, was quickly becoming obsolete, given the rising computerization of American industry (a trend whose beginning he dates to the late 1950s and early 1960s). He argued that civil rights leaders who focused on civil rights legislation alone had it all wrong. The real issue, Willhelm said, was equal employment opportunity with equal pay.

> Since the introduction of automation during the 1950s, White America has been able to expound its racism more fully and force an unwanted people into the ghetto as a way of life. Increasingly, the Negro faces the alternative of passive acceptance of the ghetto fate or taking the initiative by resorting to confrontations against White America.

Willhelm went on to describe these potential confrontations as "racial warfare" or riots. It would take nearly a decade of Black frustration with declining employment options before Willhelm's predictions became reality in the Miami riots of 1980. On December 17, 1979, thirty-three-year-old Arthur McDuffie was beaten to death by police following a moving violation. Six months later, an all-white jury found the officers involved innocent of all charges. Young Blacks in Miami's Liberty City area exploded.

In 1980, the oldest hip-hop generationers were in their early teens. The bulk of the young Black Miami rioters were born at the end of the baby boom years, but the conditions that would face the hip-hop generation were already in place—the oppression of police brutality alongside the daily injustices of poverty, unemployment, and inferior education. The 1980 riot left fourteen dead and 400 injured and caused $100 million in damages. It took 3,000 National Guardsmen to end the three days of rioting. Smaller riots, initiated by almost identical circumstances would follow in Miami in 1983,

1984, and 1989. Similar conditions faced most of America's cities, but it would take another decade before our generation would be hit hardest. By then, conditions facing Black youth had only worsened with the advancing global economy. The Los Angeles riots of 1992, the largest and most destructive American urban riot of the century, emerged as the definitive social protest event of the 1990s and signaled the impact the changing economy was having on America's poor.

Similar to the riots in Miami, Los Angeles exploded when a mostly white jury found four Los Angeles police officers innocent of the most serious charges for their beating of Black motorist Rodney King. The trial was unique in that the prosecution's case was built on an amateur video of the King beating, which was played repeatedly on news programs across the country. As in Miami, the National Guard was deployed to quell the rioting. The 2,000 National Guardsmen were inadequate, however, and were joined by 5,000 federal troops called up by President George Bush, in addition to 7,800 Los Angeles police officers. The riots lasted several days, left fifty-two dead and 2,000 injured, and caused $1 billion in damages. The 1992 Los Angeles riot became the signpost of our generation's employment woes, highlighting for the nation the social problems that decades of high unemployment, high poverty rates, limited job options, inadequate education, and pay inequality had intensified, if not produced:

1. Class Warfare. In the 1960s, urban riots were motivated primarily by Black/white social inequalities. Most of these riots, like those since, were sparked by incidents of police brutality. But unlike today, much of the rioting in those years occurred in a climate in which civil rights/Black power generationers were in search of social justice. The worst of the 1960s rioting followed the assassination of Martin Luther King Jr. and signaled a movement away from nonviolent civil disobedience. Whereas the 1960s protests were primarily concerned with racial inequality, the Los Angeles riots in 1992 revealed an intensified focus on class, in addition to racial injustice.

Many of the rioters and looters were young men, and most were Black, but whites, Latinos, women, and children were also involved. Although some whites were targeted by rioters for physical attack (what some rioters saw as a sort of payback for the Rodney King beating), all business owners in the vicinity of the rioting—Black, white, Latino, and Asian—came under attack. Undoubtedly, this level of class solidarity was elevated by the lack of employment options for hip-hop generationers. Further evidence that this generation's class consciousness transcended race appeared in the strategic attacks in downtown Los Angeles: the guardhouse outside police headquarters was set afire; fires were set inside city hall; and the city courthouse was vandalized. Rioting in San Francisco, Atlanta, and Seattle, though on a smaller scale, revealed that the discontent was a national phenomenon.

2. Police Brutality.   Far more than any other generation, the hip-hop generation was the one for which Blackness became synonymous with drugs and crime. Jimmie Lynn Reeves and Richard Campbell reported in their *Cracked Coverage: Television News, the Anti-Cocaine Crusade, and the Reagan Legacy* (Duke University Press, 1994) that in 1980 only ten cocaine-related news stories appeared on network news programs. Five years later, the number catapulted to 140 a year. Many of these stories focused on Black crime in center cities and highlighted America's fear of the Black criminal. The now infamous Willie Horton-ization of the George Bush presidential campaign was a reflection of this trend. This mentality, along with the crack explosion and the decline of decent-paying low-skilled jobs, helped to usher in a style of policing that targeted Black urban communities and which went hand in hand with police brutality.

Police brutality is not unique to the hip-hop generation; it has a long history in Black communities. In 1966, the indignity of police brutality helped summon the Black Panther Party for Self-Defense into existence. As policing efforts focused on stopping the illegal drug trade and curbing gang activity in the 1980s and 1990s, incidents of police brutality escalated in Black and Latino urban communities. From Boston to Los Angeles, from Chicago to Miami, and in numerous cities in between, incidents of young Blacks killed and beaten by police under questionable circumstances abound.

For hip-hop generationers ourselves often on the receiving end of such encounters, police brutality serves as a constant reminder of the days of Black enslavement in America. In 1857, the U.S. Supreme Court ruled in *Dred Scott v. Stanford* that Blacks "had no rights that a white man was bound to respect." In the 1990s, a vastly more sophisticated technological era, several of these incidents have been captured on video tape. Even with this see-it-yourself evidence of police brutality, predominantly white juries have found police officers to be innocent of any crime. The belief among hip-hop generationers that *injustice* will prevail has strongly influenced our generation's attitude toward policing, adding to the tension between police officers (even Black ones) and young Black civilians.

3. The Explosion of Gangs and Drugs.   Many of those pushed out of the mainstream economy take refuge in street gangs. For many both in and outside of street gangs and cliques, selling drugs is one of the most viable "job" options in the face of limited meaningful employment. Even at the height of the 1980s economic expansion, according to a 1989 survey conducted by economists Richard Freeman and Lawrence Katz (The Boston Youth Survey, National Bureau of Economic Research), more than half of young Black men felt that they could do better financially in the underground economy than in the mainstream economy. High imprisonment rates due to increased policing focused on drug crimes have landed nearly 1 million Black men, many of them hip-hop generationers, behind bars. The crack explosion of the 1980s further heightened middle-class fears of Black violent crime. Despite higher rates of monthly drug use among whites, lawmakers insisted on more concentrated policing in Black communities.

At the same time, gangs have become structurally more sophisticated in the past two decades due to high imprisonment rates of gang members and worsening economic conditions. According to the U.S. Department of Justice, by 1998, the influence of street gangs had touched every state and was as much homegrown in suburban and rural areas as it was imported from major cities. The growing availability of guns and the American gun lobby's continuing resistance to gun control allowed for wider availability of guns and further strengthened gangs and drug dealing. These dynamics, combined with the growing sophistication of gang structures, strengthened the underground economy and made drug dealing an even more viable alternative.

4. The Generation Gap.   The Black participants in the Los Angeles riots were primarily hip-hop generationers. As mainstream politicians called for calm and a strong show of force to restore law and order, many old-guard Blacks leaders (such as then Mayor Tom Bradley and NAACP executive director Benjamin Hooks) did the same. They, as well as many of our parents, quickly discovered that their advice and opinions were at odds with the rioters' beliefs. Some

Black leaders calling for calm in the wake of the Rodney King verdict also came under verbal and physical attack. One group of church members at South Central's First Episcopal Church reported being shot at by a band of young Blacks. Similar intergenerational head-butting emerged in Cincinnati during rioting in April 2001. The lasting image of NAACP head Kweisi Mfume coming to town and calling for calm but bringing no concrete solutions went down in many of our memories as a significant part of the problem in the first place.

These events marked a critical abyss between the older civil rights generation and the younger hip-hop generation. The civil rights/Black power generation grew up with a harsh, overt racism and has not been surprised by contemporary America's racial contradictions. The civil rights/Black power generation experienced segregation and second-class citizenship firsthand. Although progress has been made, the older generation realizes that institutional racism lingers. In contrast, the hip-hop generation was socialized on a steady diet of American democracy and the promise of the American dream. We grew up with television sit-coms, film, and advertisements that portrayed it as a reality. Lip service to equality, civil rights, freedom of movement, and integrated schools and neighborhoods created high expectations for our generation—even if we didn't experience it firsthand. Rodney King's color-coded justice was a slap in the face to racial equality for African Americans, revealing a double standard that few could deny.

At the same time, the older generation can't entirely identify with the mode of oppression facing our generation. Oppression for us is not simply a line in the sand with white supremacists blocking access—us over here and them over there. Because of these differing perceptions, we often see our parents themselves (and their peers) as the enemy within. Poverty, unemployment, and limited job options, as they play out in alternate ways for our generation, further feed this divide; our parents' generation views poverty as simply something many of them overcame. "Why can't your generation do the same?" or "Why does your generation use poverty as an excuse?" they ask.

5. Racial Animosity. Black inferiority (mostly based on college entrance exam scores) is often used in public discussion and debate to justify Black unemployment rates. Likewise, Black inferiority (in the form of affirmative action recipients who take "white" seats in America's colleges and "white" jobs in corporate America) is blamed for rising unemployment and poverty among whites. In the media and within policy debates, notions of Black progress and the new (but fragile) Black middle class are used to explain away contrasting high rates of unemployment, poor educational opportunities, unfair housing practices, and so forth. And in the era of downsizing, affirmative action rather than a changing economy has been viewed by angry white guys who lost jobs in the early 1990s as the culprit. Meanwhile, the rebellious "don't-give-a-fuck" self-portrait of many young Blacks in popular culture (primarily in rap music lyrics, videos, and film) has been consumed as definitive and authentic. All fuel racial animosity and hatred, even within a generation in which the races have more reason than ever to bridge the gaps between them.

America's immigrants are also privy to this berating of African Americans. A racially biased justice system only further complicates these problems. The racist attacks on whites by Blacks during the Los Angeles rioting, the targeting of Korean businesses for vandalism and looting, and the shoot-to-kill response of white police officers and white and Korean business owners reflect the deep racial divisions in our society. Each of these groups' perceptions were informed by public discussion of unemployment and education that is often out of context and focused on sensational race baiting rather than serious examination and correction of the economic and social root causes.

6. Deferment of the American Dream.   In this age of global economics, advertisements are ubiquitous. According to TV-Free America, in 1988, corporations spent $100 million on advertising aimed at children alone. By 1998, the amount spent on advertising aimed at children rose to $2 billion. The distance between the American dream as presented in the mass media and the degree to which it is increasingly unattainable for most Americans helped to fuel the Los Angeles riots. Unemployment rates, employment options, and educational preparedness among hip-hop generationers predetermine, in many cases, how we fare socially, economically, and politically.

For many, the prospects are limited. A 1991 Federal Reserve Board study of more than 6 million loan applications from 9,300 American banks nationwide revealed that Blacks were two to three times more likely than whites of similar income to be denied mortgage financing. The same disparity was true for wealthy Blacks compared to lower-income whites. In 1998, following a report from the Federal Reserve that showed that nearly 60 percent of Blacks who applied for home mortgage loans were denied, the NAACP challenged the Justice Department and Congress to investigate the lending industry's continuing discriminatory practices. Similarly, although demographic data on banks' commercial borrowers aren't made public, Blacks have long complained of the difficulty in obtaining loans to start their own businesses. Many young Blacks (conscious of how we fare compared to America's other racial and ethnic groups, despite coming to America before most) are envious of recent immigrants who set up businesses in Black communities, some of whom refuse to hire young Blacks and treat us poorly. At the same time, the daily images of an America that many of us don't experience are shoved down our throats through consumer culture. This only heightens the sense of powerlessness that many young hip-hop generationers feel. Thus, some of the rioting was sparked by the anger and frustration of being mistreated and locked out. Other episodes were marked by a carnival-like atmosphere, where the goal was to secure material goods, objects of American wealth like personal computers, televisions, stereos, appliances, furniture, clothing, and so on.

The Los Angeles riots were not solutions to these problems. Rather, the rioting, looting, and racial violence highlighted these deep-rooted social problems. Of course, racial inequities in America are not specific to this generation. But the extreme nature of these inequities in a post-segregation, post–civil rights America is specific to the hip-hop generation.

THE WORK ETHIC OF THE HIP-HOP GENERATION

Mainstream political debate and public policy from the late 1990s to the present suggests that racism is over and that any failure on the part of young Blacks to compete in today's economy is due to their own inadequacies. This rhetoric was accompanied by arguments of Black genetic inferiority that resurfaced in the 1990s (most notably Richard Herrnstein and Charles Murray's *The Bell Curve: Intelligence and Class Structure in American Life* [Free Press, 1994]) and the crusades to end social programs like affirmative action and welfare. Sensationalized media reporting about Black success during the robust economy only contributed further to the sea of misinformation about the hip-hop generation.

For example, Ellis Cose's *Newsweek* cover story, "The Good News About Black America" (June 7, 1999) relied on man-on-the-street interviews, opinion polls about how Black people *feel* they are doing, and whites' acceptance of Black professional entertainers, athletes, and celebrity leaders as their heroes to conclude that "now is a great time—the best time ever—to be Black in America." Sylvia Nasar's *New York Times* piece, "Booming Economy Draws Black Men into Fold" (May 23, 1999), used a Harvard study of 322 metropolitan areas, which found that Black men ages 16–24 with a high school education or less were more likely to be working and earning more in the later 1990s than in the early 1990s, to suggest that Blacks were doing well in the new economy. Both articles came on the heels of an April 1999 Labor Department report that indicated that the unemployment rate for Blacks was at its lowest level since 1972. Articles like these reinforce the popular mythology that the continuing high Black unemployment rate (which even at its lowest level was twice that of whites) is either make-believe, business as usual, or insignificant in the everyday lives of Black Americans. The racial disparity in these rates is generally ignored. All of this has sharply influenced public opinion and partly explains the country's failure to ameliorate the dismal record of Black unemployment.

The long-term effects of high unemployment problems on this generation, alongside being saddled with a great deal of negative baggage about our self-worth, have yet to be seen. Those at the front end of the generation are just approaching their mid-thirties. But year after year of living at or beneath the poverty line and year after year of seeing relatives, friends, and associates caught up in the underground economy and in the criminal justice system can only have reverberating effects for us, our children, and our communities.

Despite this discouraging situation, many hip-hop generationers still believe that they can achieve the American Dream. But the dream for our generation is breeding a growing and unprecedented dissatisfaction because of the consumer culture we've grown up with. Everyone wants to make it big. For many, the American Dream means not just living comfortably but becoming an overnight millionaire while still young. Many of us can't imagine waiting until we are forty, or even thirty-five, for that matter. This desire for wealth is accompanied by a sense of entitlement. That a handful of widely celebrated hip-hop generationers have achieved the dream makes the possibility real, despite the odds. Professional athletes and entertainers routinely secure million-dollar contracts. E-commerce and computer technology has also produced young millionaires seemingly overnight. It's nearly impossible to find a kid on the block who doesn't think he can be the next Puff Daddy or Master P, Chris Webber or Tiger Woods. Although such attitudes existed in previous generations, with the hip-hop generation, it is a near obsession. And this desire to achieve not simply financial security but millionaire status is the driving force of our generation's work ethic.

This is not to say that hip-hop generationers expect to bypass hard work as a prerequisite. Young Blacks, like most Americans, when given the opportunity to work, have demonstrated their willingness to do so. In one sociological study of inner-city poverty after another, countless teenagers and twenty-somethings describe working long hours to make ends meet. Many (like their counterparts in the military) work more than one job. Some supplement their low-wage, no-benefits job with some sort of underground economy hustle, adding even more hours to an already long workday. Anthropologist Katherine Newman in her 1999 book *No Shame in My Game: The Working Poor in the Inner City* (Knopf and the Russell Sage Foundation, 1999) documents hundreds of low-skilled Black and Latino workers in Harlem who demonstrate a willingness to work. The key is hope and possibility.

Rappers from working-poor backgrounds often work long hours in recording studios, giving concerts, making music videos, and so on. Aspiring and self-published rappers selling their CDs in local and regional markets do the same. With rap music as a concrete and legitimate employment option, they have something to believe in and are working in an area where they receive a sense of personal worth and satisfaction. In the wake of the Los Angeles riots, the Crips and the Bloods signed a truce and penned a manifesto that ended with, "Give us the hammer and the nails and we will rebuild the city." This is the work ethic that this generation espouses. Yet at every turn, obstacles stand in the way. Those young Blacks who overcome them do so against great odds. Their perseverance should be applauded, but their examples don't render the societal obstacles irrelevant.

The civil rights and Black power movements won the war for legal access and laid the foundation for philosophical and cultural change. The war for economic access for a majority of Black Americans has yet to be won, however. The call for a Black economic agenda that revives Black communities and puts young Blacks into long-term jobs has yet to be answered. Since the mid-1970s, the National Urban League has issued an annual report, *The State of Black America.* That report has long been calling for a Marshall Plan for America's cities. Year after year the report has sounded the alarm of the desperate plight of center-city Black America, especially young Blacks. Sociologist William Julius Wilson noted in the 1998 report of *The State of Black America* that if the commitment is to the poor rather than to Blacks alone, Americans will be more willing to cooperate. Rather than rise to the challenge, policy makers have tended to ignore these calls for action.

It is not as though opportunities do not exist for economic development. Urban school districts experiencing teacher shortages, say in math and science, are recruiting teachers abroad rather than establishing teacher training programs for jobless citizens at home. Likewise, in Silicon Valley, many corporations recruit Japanese, Chinese, and Indian nationals to fill high-skilled jobs rather than training young Blacks at home. This pattern has been repeated in many other industries through the use of the government's H1B visa program, which by 2000 had allowed U.S. companies to import 425,000 skilled workers plus their dependents. The roots of such practices are historical and demonstrate the country's failure both in the public and private sectors to commit itself to employment of its own citizenry. This is an American problem. The question of reparations can again place it on the table of national discussion.

Until these employment issues are addressed, Black youth must continue to explore creative options. Perhaps it is time for another Great Migration, but in reverse. Older Blacks, some of whom led the charge out of the South to Northern cities in the 1950s and 1960s, realize that America's big cities do not hold the promise they once did; jobless, crime-ridden ghettos have become glorified, modern-day concentration camps. Many older Blacks have begun the move out of Northern cities. Some are looking forward to retirement, but most of those returning to their rural, Southern roots are in their forties and fifties. According to a 1997 migration analysis by U.S. Agriculture Department geographer John Cromartie, the South regained more than 500,000 Blacks lost to the North during the Great Migration, most of whom are blue-collar workers. Most young Blacks, drawn to the aura of big city life, have yet to catch on. Yet some in the high-skilled job market realize they must go where the jobs are and are moving away from family and friends to secure a higher standard of living. This strategy needs to be translated into a working policy for low-skilled workers until they obtain the skills needed to compete for higher-paying jobs. The future for Blacks, young or old, in the ghettos of America's cities is severely limited as long as these communities remain as they are.

Until there is a serious commitment to economic development, equal access, and a level playing field, hip-hop generationers will continue to be subject to inferior schools, limited employment possibilities, and lifestyles out of sync with the best of what America has to offer its citizens. It became popular during the Clinton administration to lament the digital divide—the idea that Blacks were being left behind due to their limited access to computer technology. That divide, and its economic consequences, will persist for African Americans as long as disparities in employment, education, training, and development continue to exist.

As significant as the hip-hop generation's unemployment problem is, it is only compounded for a growing number of young Black men and women who have been locked out of this game altogether. Their fate as federal, state, and county prison inmates is the subject of the next chapter.

3

RACE WAR

Policing, Incarceration, and the Containment of Black Youth

THERE'S A WAR GOING ON OUTSIDE
NO MAN IS SAFE FROM
YOU CAN RUN BUT YOU CAN'T HIDE FOREVER.
— MOBB DEEP, "SURVIVAL OF THE FIT"

ON APRIL 20, 1995, U.S. ATTORNEY JAMES BURNS AND COOK County's Illinois State Attorney Jack O'Malley held a press conference to announce the indictments of twenty-three members of the Traveling Vice Lords for federal drug conspiracy charges. An additional eight members of the Chicago street gang, including several juveniles, were indicted on separate state narcotics or weapons charges. Authorities alleged that the gang ran a crack cocaine and heroin market that netted anywhere from $5,000 to $30,000 a day. The gang operated what prosecutors described as one of the city's most lucrative open-air drug markets in the 2700 block of West Flourney Street in Chicago's East Garfield Park neighborhood. "We have taken down one of the major street gang, drug-dealing factions in the city," Burns said.

The three-and-a-half-year sting operation, dubbed Operation Flourney, which led to the arrests, began in July of 1991 and joined Chicago police forces with the ATF and the FBI. However, this herculean effort culminated with the seizure of only four and one-half pounds of powder cocaine at the apartment of the alleged gang leader, Andrew "Bay-Bay" Patterson, and less than $2,000 from two other defendants. Only several gold chains, a watch, and beepers were seized from the remaining defendants. Despite the limited physical evidence, the criminal charges were based on prosecutors' claims that the gang made as much as $24,000 a day from selling crack cocaine in 1994. Further, prosecutors alleged that in 1995, when members started dealing heroin, too, they doubled their daily cash intake.

One year later, nineteen of those indicted for conspiracy were tried simultaneously. Most of the defendants were hip-hop generationers, ranging from twenty-one to forty-one years old. The case had the largest number of defendants for a single trial in the history of the Northern District of Illinois Court. In June 1996, after a trial that lasted five months, fifteen of the defendants were convicted of federal drug conspiracy charges. The remaining four defendants were acquitted. Two of those four were returned to state custody to finish serving sentences on weapons and drug charges. Due to federal sentencing guidelines and mandatory minimum sentencing laws, none of those convicted were sentenced to less than seventeen and one-half years. Three received life sentences.

Operation Flourney offers a glimpse into young Blacks' involvement in the criminal justice system and the type of criminal charges and state and federal laws that have landed a disproportionate number of young Blacks behind bars during the past two decades. The lengthy mandatory minimum prison sentences for drug crimes, coupled with the general drug prohibition hysteria focused on urban (read: Black and Latino) communities that has come to dominate law enforcement at local, state, and federal levels, are characteristic of the 1980s and 1990s. The end result has been the prison crisis, a crisis that has profoundly influenced our generation.

The war on drugs is the focal point for this crisis. In our lifetime, the population incarcerated in U.S. state and federal prisons and local jails has climbed from fewer than 200,000 in 1965 to nearly 2 million today. According to the Bureau of Justice, approximately 50 percent of federal and state prisoners are African American, a startling imbalance. Consider the statistics. According to a 1997 survey by the Substance Abuse and Mental Health Services Administration, Blacks make up only 13 percent of monthly illegal drug users, whereas whites constitute 74 percent of monthly illegal drug users. Yet, in 1995, the National Criminal Justice Commission reported that 74 percent of those sentenced to prison for drug possession were Black. At the state level, which houses the bulk of America's prisoners, the Justice Department found that the number of Blacks incarcerated for drug offenses increased 707 percent during the decade between 1985 and 1995 (compared to a 306 percent increase for whites). By 1996, drug offenders made up 23 percent of the state inmate population and 60 percent of the federal incarcerated population. Of all drug offenders admitted to state prisons in 1996, according to the 2000 Human Rights Report ("Punishment and Prejudice: Racial Disparities in the War on Drugs"), 62.6 percent were Black, and 36.7 percent were white.

These statistics reveal that race is clearly a factor. Approximately 1 million Black men are currently under some form of correctional supervision. And the hip-hop generation is suffering the greatest casualties; approximately one-third of all Black males age 20–29 are incarcerated, or on probation, or on parole. In the past two decades, few issues have altered Black life as much as the incarceration of young Blacks.

MANDATORY MINIMUMS

For their drug crimes, the fifteen former residents of the 2700 block of South Flourney received sentences determined under federal sentencing guidelines and mandatory minimum sentencing laws, which went into effect in the 1980s, some established under the 1980s provisions tacked onto the 1970 Racketeering Influenced Corrupt Organization Act (RICO) and the 1970 Continuing Criminal Enterprise Act (CCE). As noted above, none were sentenced to anything less than seventeen and one-half years. The youngest defendant, twenty-one-year-old Andrew L. "Maine" Patterson, who prosecutors said was an enforcer for the gang, was sentenced to twenty-five years and ten months. He would have received life imprisonment under mandatory minimum sentencing laws, but Judge Robert Gettleman said that police failed in their responsibility under Illinois' Juvenile Court Act (which gives police authority to take into custody without a warrant any minor they have reasonable cause to believe is living in an "injurious environment") to turn him over to juvenile authorities when they discovered he was involved in dealing illegal drugs in 1991. At that time, Andrew was only fifteen, but law enforcers claimed that turning him over to juvenile authorities would have compromised the investigation. Federal sentencing guidelines allowed Gettleman to lower the sentence. The harshest sentences were meted out to Bay-Bay Patterson, Robert Patterson, and Tyrone Williams, each of whom received life imprisonment, required by mandatory minimum sentencing laws.

The origin of mandatory minimum sentences (commonly referred to as mandatory minimums) in the United States can be traced back to the 1951 Boggs Act, which imposed mandatory minimum sentences for drug crimes, and the 1956 Boggs Act enhancements, which increased sentences established in the 1951 law. In 1970, Congress threw out the mandatory minimum sentences established in the 1950s because small-time dealers and addicts were receiving sentences meant for big-time dealers, a problem that present-day opponents of mandatory minimums insist we are now repeating. Nevertheless, by the early 1970s some state legislatures began to establish minimum sentencing laws of their own, the most notable of which are New York State's 1973 Rockefeller drug laws. New York's law requires that anyone convicted of selling more than two ounces of cocaine, heroin, or other controlled substances—or possessing more than four ounces—be sentenced to a minimum of fifteen years in prison. Other states subsequently passed their own mandatory minimum sentencing drug laws. But it was a series of federal laws passed by Congress in the mid-eighties that brought into existence the current federal mandatory minimum sentencing for drug crimes.

In 1984, the Comprehensive Crime Control Act was passed. This law established five-year mandatory minimums for using or carrying a gun during drug or violent crimes, in addition to the sentence for the initial crime. Further, a fifteen-year mandatory minimum sentence was created for possession of a gun by a person with three previous state or federal convictions for burglary or robbery. Also established in 1984 was the Sentencing Reform Act, which phased out the seventy-five-year-old federal parole system. At the same time, the U.S. Sentencing Commission was established to create guidelines that would make sentences for the same crime uniform. It also determined how long one could be locked up for a specific crime. This commission is responsible for what are popularly referred to as the federal sentencing guidelines, a small range of sentences for each category of offense. The sentencing judge selects from this range at the time of sentencing. The guidelines, which went into effect in November 1987, limit judges' discretion and give prosecutors so great a role in the sentencing process that many point to this as one of the major changes in the criminal justice system in the last two decades.

In 1986, under the Anti-Drug Abuse Act, Congress established new federal mandatory minimums for offenses related to the most frequently used illegal drugs. Five-year mandatory minimums were created for distributing and importing specific quantities of illegal drugs. Heavily focused on crack cocaine, the bill established a 100 to 1 sentencing ratio between crack and powder cocaine and enacted a death penalty for drug "kingpins."

More mandatory minimums for drug offenses were added with the passage of the 1988 Omnibus Anti-Drug Abuse Act, particularly for crack cocaine possession and conspiracy convictions. Additionally, Congress extended the net for who could be tried for conspiracy, regardless of how central or peripheral the offender. A five-year mandatory minimum was established for simple possession of more than five grams of crack cocaine, whereas possession of the same amount of other drugs, including powder cocaine, remained misdemeanors with mandatory minimums of fifteen days for the second offense. Also under the law, the ten-year mandatory minimum for engaging in a continuing criminal enterprise—a concept originally introduced in 1970—was doubled to twenty years.

More than a decade and hundreds of thousands of convictions later, including those of many hip-hop generationers, the Supreme Court ruled in a 6–3 decision in June 1999 that a prosecutor trying a defendant on continuing criminal enterprise violations must convince the jury that the accused both committed each of the individual violations and committed them in a continuing series. But between

1988 and June 1999, prosecutors had only had to convince jurors that defendants had broken the law three times or that they had committed one or two violations in a series but not necessarily the third.

Finally, in 1994, California enacted an even more stringent sentencing law—what has come to be known as "three strikes and you're out." It requires mandatory life imprisonment for a third felony conviction. Since then, at least twenty states have passed similar measures. In addition, 1994 saw the passage of the federal crime bill, which required states to mandate that offenders serve a minimum of 85 percent of their sentences (dubbed Truth in Sentencing) in order for states to qualify for federal funding for prisons.

Collectively, these laws enacted between 1984 and 1994, along with state mandatory minimums for drug crimes, more than anything else, helped to give the United States the world's largest inmate population and the world's second-highest per capita incarceration rate. This wave of mandatory minimum laws was part of a legislative and judicial process that became more and more anti-youth in the 1980s and 1990s, and it has wreaked havoc on the hip-hop generation. Although the crack cocaine explosion of the 1980s had created a surge of violent crime in such cities as New York City, Chicago, Los Angeles, St. Louis, and Washington, D.C., which contributed to the climate that allowed for the passage of these laws, crime rates had begun to decrease across the country by 1992. Despite these declines, imprisonment has continued to soar, with drug offenders making up one out of every four U.S. prisoners.

"TESTILYING" AND CORRUPTION

Located on the notorious West Side of Chicago, East Garfield Park was once a vibrant community that as early as the

1920s boasted thriving commercial activity and employment opportunities. Although some industries began moving out in the mid-1930s, the then mostly white community continued to enjoy good times. The arrival of many working-class Black families in the 1950s drove the population to its height of 70,000, with Blacks representing 17 percent. However, the 1968 riots (in response to the assassination of Martin Luther King Jr.) devastated the community's economic life. These riots, like those in many Black urban communities around the country in the late 1960s, coincided with a decline in economic activity and a migration of industry and jobs, along with white residents, to America's suburbs. By the 1990s, countless condemned and abandoned buildings, alongside vacant lots, had replaced the merchants' shops of the earlier era, as East Garfield Park's population plummeted to a 24,000, mostly Black population. At least 46 percent of the neighborhood's families were living at the poverty level at the time of Operation Flourney.

All of the young men who made up what prosecutors referred to as "the Patterson family enterprise" lived on or around the 2700 block of South Flourney. Prosecutors initially claimed they were all members of the Traveling Vice Lords. However sensational this sounded to the press and however well it supported the conspiracy and racketeering charges, not all of the men were gang members. Some were relatives; some were lifetime acquaintances. Several of the men were drug addicts, several were alcoholics, and others were small-time dealers. Although none of the defendants testified in this case, their attorneys never disputed that their clients sold drugs. Although all the defendants were taped discussing drugs and drug selling, none were arrested in the process of selling drugs, and only one was arrested with drugs in his possession. During the trial, officer Bob Drozd, one of the prosecution's key witnesses, testified that he "never saw any drug dealing going on" on Flourney because if he had, he "would have arrested these boys." The defense, however, did deny that the operation was as lucrative as prosecutors said it was, and they denied that the defendants were part of an elaborate conspiracy. Operation Flourney caught in its web most of the young men who lived on the block. This nabbing of acquaintances, some of whom may have been far on the periphery of whatever drug dealing was going on, and charging them as co-conspirators is typical of how CCE and RICO laws are being used to prosecute young Blacks around the country, some of whom are members of well-organized Black street gangs but many of whom are not hard-core gang members at all.

The federal government's case against "the Patterson family" relied heavily on the testimony of undercover police officer Bob Drozd. Officer Drozd, a fifty-three-year-old gang crimes specialist, spent countless hours secretly tape-recording more than 250 tapes of conversations with Andrew Bay-Bay Patterson and the other defendants. Drozd's tapes were used by prosecutors not only to identify those involved in the conspiracy but also to determine the quantity of drugs being sold. Drozd was also responsible for transcribing the tapes. In places where the tapes are unintelligible, prosecutors relied on Drozd's memory to fill in the blanks.

According to Drozd, who says he was working undercover as a corrupt and drug-addicted cop, the dealers traded him guns and drugs for his agreeing not to interfere and keeping other officers from interfering with drug sales. However, only thirty-four guns were recovered over the entire three-and-a-half-year investigation. It was the hope of seizing guns that got the Bureau of Alcohol, Tobacco, and Firearms (ATF) involved. In early 1991, the AFT had reason to believe that the Traveling Vice Lords were buying guns from a Clarksdale, Mississippi, gun dealer. The ATF assigned an agent to work with the Chicago Police Department in hopes of uncovering a major arsenal of weapons used by the Vice Lords to protect their drug operations. No arsenal was ever found, and none of the thirty-four guns taken in by the investigation were new.

Rather naively, the defendants hoped that jurors would realize that Drozd's testimony could not be trusted. This would be enough, they thought, to free them of most of the charges and from draconian mandatory sentencing. Thus, defense attorneys painted a picture of Drozd as an alcoholic, racist, extortionist, corrupt cop whose testimony was untrustworthy and should not be admissible. They argued that Drozd had a history of alcohol abuse. Drozd himself testified that during the investigation he was drinking anywhere from a twelve pack to a case of beer a day. He also admitted that he had entered a program to combat his drinking problem in April 1994. Defense attorneys argued that Drozd was also a drug addict and a racist, citing a white supremacist tattoo. More importantly, defense attorneys argued, the tapes did not reveal bribery on the part of the defendants, as the prosecution had claimed, but rather extortion by Officer Drozd.

Whether or not Drozd was indeed corrupt is disputable. What the Patterson case makes clear, however, is that in this age of prohibition, dirty cops are par for the course; the defendants saw nothing wrong with bribing him if (as the prosecution claimed) it was bribery or giving into extortion if (as the defense claimed) Drozd was in fact shaking them down. In the war on drugs, both are considered business as usual. According to the FBI, between 1994 and 1997, 508 officers were convicted in federal corruption cases. And the corruption isn't isolated to big cities; the officers convicted came from forty-seven cities, large and small, from coast to coast.

Consider the 1994–1996 Cleveland police corruption investigation, which led to federal corruption charges against forty-four law enforcement officers, including sheriff's department deputies, sheriff's department corrections officers, and members of the Cleveland Police Department as well as other regional police departments. The ring of corrupt officers regularly provided security for illegal drug deals. According to federal prosecutors, officers were paid $750–$3,700 per transaction. Sixteen such deals were captured on video and audio tape by undercover agents, where officers served as escorts and security guards for agents they believed were cocaine dealers.

Also in 1994, city, state, and federal sting operations into New York City Police Department's 30th Precinct revealed thirty-three officers—or one-sixth of the precinct—who participated in selling cocaine, robbing drug dealers of guns, drugs, and cash, conducting illegal raids, or committing perjury to secure convictions. The activities earned the precinct the name "Dirty Thirty." Perjury was so commonplace that officers came to refer to it as "testilying." Prosecutors later identified 2,000 cases where the officers' testimony tainted the evidence. By 1997, at least 125 convictions were overturned against ninety-eight defendants, as their convictions were based on the corrupt officers' testimony. Some of these victims sued New York City for unlawful imprisonment and won settlements that totaled at least $1.3 million by 1997.

In New Orleans, twelve police officers were convicted of cocaine conspiracy charges for running a cocaine protection ring. The officers were nabbed in an FBI investigation into police corruption, called Operation Shattered Shield, between December 1993 and December 1994. The group of officers provided security for a drug warehouse, which they didn't realize was actually run by FBI agents. What pushed this case into national headlines, however, was not the corruption but the role of Officer Len Davis, who went so far as to order a hit on a woman who filed a police brutality complaint against him. Less than twenty-four hours after Davis learned that Kim Groves had complained about his involvement in brutality against a neighborhood teen, Len Davis ordered her killed by a drug dealer acquaintance. Beyond the cocaine conspiracy charges, Davis was also convicted of murder.

More relevant to the case against the Patterson family is Operation Broken Star, a federal investigation into police corruption on Chicago's West Side. In 1997, federal narcotics charges against several officers grew out of Operation Flourney. During the testimony in the 1995 trial, Dixmoor Park District officer Terry Young, thirty-one, was said to be a co-leader with Bay-Bay Patterson of the Traveling Vice Lords. According to prosecutors, Young and another officer from the Austin District—who was allegedly a high-ranking member of another faction of the Vice Lords, the Conservative Vice Lords—worked together in robbing other drug dealers of drugs and money. Seven cops were charged with robbing an undercover agent who was pretending to be a drug dealer. Young was also charged along with thirteen others with running a cocaine and heroin operation at Henry Horner Homes and Rockwell Gardens public housing developments.

POLICING YOUNG BLACKS

These incidents are not isolated cases. Officers routinely operate above the law in policing Black communities, and this corrupt mentality permeates law enforcement in general. The style of policing in these communities is often war-like in appearance, not by coincidence but by design. Leading the charge are paramilitary or tactical policing units—divisions of the police department that are trained to deal with hostage situations, bomb threats, suicide attempts, and the apprehension of murder suspects. However, they are used primarily in urban communities to serve drug warrants, carry out raids, and in some cases, conduct street patrols, stopping mostly young citizens for minor offenses and arresting them for drug possession or outstanding warrants. Their reinvention inspired by the crack explosion of the mid-1980s and police fear of being outgunned by warring drug dealing factions, paramilitary units initially took their cue from the Special Weapons and Tactics (SWAT) units of an earlier era. (The Los Angeles Police Department gave the country its first paramilitary unit—the brainchild of LAPD's Darryl Gates of 1992 L.A. riots notoriety.) The original goal was to suppress race riots that had become routine in the late 1960s. Ironically, they have turned from one type of race war to another.

According to a 1997 study by Eastern Kentucky University sociologist Peter Kraska titled "Militarizing American Police: The Rise and Normalization of Paramilitary Units," there are more than 30,000 of these units currently operating in the United States. Kraska says that the percentage of police departments with paramilitary units increased from 59 percent in 1982 to 89 percent in 1995, and annual deployments increased from 2,000 in 1980 to 31,000 in 1995. These divisions of police departments use military equipment and tactics to conduct police work involving mostly small crimes. In the process, they most certainly contribute to high arrest rates in these communities. Some of the military equipment they possess has come from the surplus of U.S. military hardware, which increased sharply after the end of the Cold War. In 1995, Congress enacted the National Defense Authorization Act, which allowed police departments to receive helicopters, Kevlar helmets, M-16s, personnel carriers, tanks, and much more for free. Between 1995 and 1997, more than $200 million worth of military equipment was handed down to state and local law enforcement agencies.

Interestingly, paramilitary units have been criticized for their use of military equipment, their style of policing, and their potential for killing innocent civilians—but not for their racist targeting of Black communities or the fact that white officers man many of these units. At the same time, there is a widely held misconception that Blacks commit the most crimes in this country, a rationalization that, for many, explains the existing disproportionate arrest and incarceration rates. This myth was debunked by two separate studies published in 2000—one by the National Council on Crime and Delinquency and one by the Leadership Conference on Civil Rights—which concur that Black and Latino youth are more likely than whites to be arrested, prosecuted, and sentenced to long prison sentences. The paramilitary units' focus on Black communities and their policing tactics, which go above and beyond the call of duty to arrest young Blacks, make it clear that higher Black arrest rates are linked to more vigilant policing.

Nothing better illustrates how racially charged this type of policing is than the November 1990 raid in Chapel Hill, North Carolina. The city's and the state's paramilitary units received a blanket search warrant for an entire block in a predominately Black neighborhood and searched every vehicle, home, and person on the block. Although more than 100 Blacks were searched, whites were allowed to leave the area. Thirteen people were arrested. Later the charges against the thirteen were dropped when the district attorney deemed the blanket search warrant too vague to enforce. In 1991, thirty-seven people filed a lawsuit against the cities of Chapel Hill and Corboro. (Officers involved in the raid were employees of these cities.) Claiming that they were assaulted and falsely imprisoned, among other charges, the plaintiffs asserted that the raid violated their constitutional rights. An out of court settlement was reached in 1996.

Constitutional rights of citizens are equally disregarded in less extreme cases of paramilitary policing. At both ends of the spectrum, police officers, units, and departments take the position that most of "them" are guilty anyway. They compile databases and conduct stops and searches looking for drug offenses and reasons to arrest. Unfortunately for hip-hop generationers, these tactics don't end with paramilitary policing. Reinforcing a mentality of what Jerome Miller calls "search and destroy" are nationwide approaches to policing in general. Miller argues that most officers, especially those policing Black communities, are already corrupt in terms of their ability to police Blacks, because they accept the assumption that Black youth are public enemy number one. This mentality spills over into narcotics units in countless police departments. Racial profiling is the direct result of this mentality.

A textbook case of rampant racial profiling is the New Jersey State Troopers' policy of random vehicle stops, a tactic used to fight drug trafficking. This practice came under attack in April 1998 following an incident in which two troopers opened fire on four young Black and Latino men after pulling them over while they were en route from New York City to North Carolina Central University for college basketball tryouts. Daniel Reyes, twenty, Rayshawn Brown, twenty, and Leroy Grant, twenty-three, all unarmed, were wounded by gunfire after their rental van began to roll backward— toward the officers—on the New Jersey Turnpike shoulder. (The fourth man, also unarmed, was not injured.) A subsequent report by the state of New Jersey reviewed random vehicle stops on the New Jersey Turnpike between July 1997 and February 1999 and found that although 59.4 percent of motorists stopped were white, 77.2 percent of those searched for drugs by state troopers were Black or Latino.

New York Police Department's Street Crimes Unit gained a similar reputation for racial profiling in the wake of the shooting death of Amadou Diallo. Four officers from the

unit fired forty-one shots, nineteen of which struck the unarmed Diallo. A subsequent investigation into the unit's activities revealed that of the 45,000 people stopped and
frisked in 1997 and 1998, only 9,500 led to arrests. The unit,
whose slogan at that time was "We Own the Night," donned
hooded sweatshirts and blue jeans and was mostly white. In
the wake of the shooting, fifty Black officers were added to
the 362-strong unit, uniforms have replaced their street
clothes, and its officers have been retrained in search and
seizure rules and racial sensitivity.

In addition to racial profiling, random parole sweeps
have become common across the country. This practice has
been particularly intrusive in New York City, where since
1997 police and parole officers have teamed up to conduct
special nighttime visits to parolees' homes who live in
"high-crime" areas (mostly housing projects) or who are
seen as possible repeat offenders. Parolees are questioned
about crimes in the area and are forced to give urine samples
for drug tests. Those who refuse are taken to the precinct for
further questioning, as are those who test positive for drug
use (a violation of their parole). Officers rely on parole agreements that allow parole officers to search parolee sleeping
areas (not the entire home) at any time. Critics like the
American Civil Liberties Union (ACLU) say such practices
constitute illegal search and seizure, as police officers generally need a search warrant to carry out the type of searches
that they conduct while piggybacking off the parole officers'
raid. The parole program also teams up parole and police officers, allowing police officers to interrogate parolees about
crimes in the area during routine parole appointments.

The philosophy that anything goes when policing
Blacks is not restricted to the local level. The search procedures of the U.S. Customs Service have recently come under
attack. Whereas police officers can search individuals and

possessions based only upon reasonable cause and with warrants, U.S. Customs Service officers at airports and border crossings have the legal authority to conduct stops and searches based upon reasonable suspicion that something illegal is being hidden. Such searches include pat-down body searches, strip searches, and in some cases, body-cavity searches by doctors while Customs officers watch. In the summer of 1998, eighty African American women (all of whom were unsuccessfully searched for drugs) filed a class action lawsuit against customs officials, charging that they were unfairly targeted for intrusive strip and body-cavity searches at Chicago's O'Hare International Airport because of their race and gender and that no legal cause existed for conducting such searches. Similar lawsuits were filed against customs officials at international airports at Fort Lauderdale-Hollywood and Tampa.

Customs officials claim that only 50,000 of the 68 million travelers whose luggage passes through customs annually are subject to personal searches. Only 1,772 passengers were strip-searched in 1997, according to U.S. Customs Service figures, and only nineteen were subject to body-cavity searches. Of the nineteen, drugs were found in twelve of the searches. Clearly the U.S. Customs Service figures on strip and body-cavity searches are far lower than those indicated by the lawsuits.

Since the legal and media onslaughts on the vague policy, customs officials have made several changes. Among other things, high-tech body search scanners have been installed at thirteen international airports, a customs customer satisfaction unit has been created, and customs lawyers have been placed on twenty-four-hour duty to advise officers conducting drug searches. As with the racial profiling of NYPD's Street Crimes Unit and New Jersey's State Troopers, it was national publicity and subsequent damage control that led to corrective action. Despite such changes, the mentality persists, and constitutional rights are routinely denied in the interest of fighting the drug war, targeting demographic segments assumed to lack the political leverage needed to resist the onslaught. Often the discrimination is cloaked with the rationalization that the local community, as society overall, welcomes it.

THE SNITCH FACTOR

State and federal drug cases like the one against the Patterson family depend not only on undercover cops but, perhaps more importantly, on informants (also known as snitches) who agree to plead guilty and testify as government witnesses in exchange for special considerations, including leniency in sentencing. According to the *National Law Journal*, the federal government alone paid roughly $500 million to informants between 1985 and 1993. Ironically, one of the few things that made the case against the Patterson family unique was that unlike most drug conspiracy cases, none of the original defendants caved in to prosecutors' bait of a lesser sentence in exchange for undermining the others and testifying that a continuing criminal enterprise actually existed. So routine is the snitch factor as a key tool in prosecuting today's drug crimes that the loyalty of the nineteen defendants to one another created a buzz among inmates housed at Chicago's Metropolitan Correctional Center during their trial.

But this didn't stop prosecutors from securing other residents from the area as informants. The prosecution unearthed three persons who they alleged were also subject to drug conspiracy charges in the case but were not included in the original indictments: Thane Martin, Johnny Robinson, and Warren Reynolds. Whether telling the truth or embellishing it, the informants' recollections of events lined up perfectly with prosecutors' charges. However, cross-examination of Thane Martin proved embarrassing for the prosecution. A self-confessed crack and heroin addict who worked as lookout and street dealer in Bay-Bay's drug-dealing operation to support his habit, Martin broke down under cross-examination and agreed with one of the defense attorneys that he was "telling lies to keep [himself] out of the penitentiary." Such moments of truth reveal the conflict of interest in using informants who stand to gain legal payoffs of cash, cars, jobs, homes, reduced sentences, and so forth, from the federal government in exchange for their cooperation, even if they may not be telling the truth. For his testimony, Martin, like Robinson, received a sentence of five to seven and a half years. (Reynolds received four years.) Due to his five previous drug convictions, Martin's alleged involvement in conspiracy had him facing life imprisonment, even though his only tangible role in the conspiracy was telling Officer Drozd where to find the initial gun, the bribe that jump-started the investigation.

Regardless of their serious credibility problems (common sense strongly suggests that individuals who are receiving something in exchange for testimony often have a motive to lie), such government witnesses have remained unchallenged tools in prosecuting drug crimes—until July 1, 1998, when a U.S. circuit court challenged the practice of prosecutors offering plea bargains in exchange for testimony of co-conspirators. Three judges of the Federal Court of Appeals for the 10th Circuit overturned the conviction of twenty-five-year-old Sonya Singleton, a Wichita, Kansas, mother of two who had been convicted of cocaine trafficking and money laundering. Judge Paul Kelly, Judge Stephanie Seymour, and Judge David Ebel ruled that the chief witness against her should not have been given leniency in his own case in exchange for his testimony against Singleton and others. Judge Paul Kelly wrote, "If justice is perverted when a criminal defendant seeks to buy testimony from a witness, it is no less perverted when the government does so."

The decision sent shock waves throughout the criminal justice system. Especially peeved were prosecutors who had come to rely on such deals more than anything else to secure convictions for drug crimes. If this drug policy were overturned, literally thousands would walk free. Not surprisingly, the war-on-drugs machine swung into action. The Justice Department appealed the decision, claiming that it would paralyze law enforcement and undermine prosecutors, and requested that it be dismissed. To persuade any naysayers, the Justice Department leaned heavily on the example of Oklahoma City bombers Timothy McVeigh and Terry Nichols, who had quickly incorporated the July ruling into their appeals. And in case the full 10th Circuit Court didn't tow the war-on-drugs party line, two bills were introduced in the Senate to amend the bribery statute, making it inapplicable to prosecutors making plea bargain agreements. Six months later, the full twelve-member 10th Circuit Court of Appeals overturned the July decision.

As in the case against the Patterson family, the use of informants in the war on drugs has turned lifetime friends, neighbors, and acquaintances against one another, as well as brother against brother. Given the extent to which the war on drugs has permeated the hip-hop generation—through high rates of arrest and conviction for drug crimes at the state and federal level—this has certainly challenged ideas of friendship, family loyalty, and community cohesiveness among this generation. Thirty-two-year-old Shavelle Dismuke, who was convicted of drug conspiracy charges in 1996 on the strength of a co-conspirator's testimony in a case without any physical evidence against him, attests to this. "They're using our own people to do the snitching," says

Dismuke, a first-time offender who's serving a twenty-year sentence for being the ringleader in a drug operation that trafficked cocaine from Jamaica to Atlanta. "They're using your cousins and brothers and friends to set you up, and it's got to stop."

Jerome Miller, president of the National Center on Institutions and Alternatives, who has directed juvenile justice systems in several states and has worked in corrections for the past three decades, agrees. According to Miller, the implications of the government's use of informants don't just stop at betrayal but extend to rising rates of intraracial Black homicide in the 1980s and 1990s. In his *Search and Destroy: African-American Males in the Criminal Justice System*, he writes: "Relying on informers threatens and eventually cripples much more than criminal enterprise. It erodes whatever social bonds exist in families, in the community, or on the streets—loyalty which, in past years, kept violence within bounds." According to the U.S. Sentencing Commission Annual Report, 19 percent of all federal cases where defendants received sentences lower than the federal guidelines in 1997 involved prosecutors' use of informant testimony.

PRISONS AND INMATE LABOR IN A GLOBAL ECONOMY

Capitalizing on the war on drugs mania is the privatized prison industry—a network of private corporations that provide every service imaginable to prisons and inmates, from prison construction and operation to telecommunications services, clothing, food, and medicine. Recognizing that U.S. taxpayers spend approximately $35 billion a year on prisons, these companies increasingly are getting a piece of the action. They have their own journals and trade shows (such as the American Correction Association Convention) like any other thriving industry, and more and more are venturing beyond state and national markets to global ones.

Corrections Corporation of America, Wakenhut Corrections Corporation, Cornell Corrections, and U.S. Corrections Corporation are at the forefront of a growing number of private companies in the business of building prisons, operating prisons, and/or housing inmates for federal and state governments for a profit. Analysts estimate that the industry is worth $1 billion a year, with more than 160 private facilities functioning in at least twenty-six states. Private prison corporations have also extended operations into England, South Africa, Australia, and parts of Central America and South America, as more countries privatize their prison systems. Some of the companies that have gone public, CCA and Wakenhut, for example, have enjoyed increases in their stock prices that parallel the explosion of technology stock that dominated the late 1990s. And just as tech start-ups offer employees stock options instead of grand salaries, private prisons offer staffers, such as guards, stock options instead of pension plans. Companies like TransCor America, the Federal Extradition Agency, and the Bobby Ross Group transport thousands of prisoners daily across state lines for a fee. Bed broker companies like Dominion Management, link up overcrowded state correctional systems in need of facilities to house their inmates with the private prisons that meet budgetary constraints.

Once a month, Henry Patterson, one of the fourteen individuals convicted in the Patterson family trial, checks in with his attorney to see if there is any movement on his appeal. Like most inmates whose only contact with the world back home is via telephone (and infrequent visitors because they are moved so far away from home), Henry must call collect. "This is an MCI collect call from a federal corrections institute. This conversation will be recorded. Caller state your name." Whether it's MCI's Maximum Security, AT&T's The Authority, or Bell South's Max, prison inmate long-distance services generally charge higher rates plus surcharges beyond the typical collect long-distance call. The competition for this business is so great that telephone companies offer prisons a hefty percentage of the profit, sometimes as much as 60 percent, in exchange for exclusive contracts.

Corporations also capitalize on cheap prison labor. Federal and state prisons once restricted prison labor to services and products made for government and nonprofit agencies. However, in 1979, Congress created the Prison Industry Enhancement certification program (CPI), which gave private companies access to prison laborers. Major corporations shopping for the cheapest labor have realized that mandatory minimum sentencing and state laws governing private industry's use of prison laborers have created a captive, non-unionized labor pool, where benefits, vacation time, unemployment compensation, minimum wages, payroll and Social Security taxes, and even human rights and anti-sweatshop activists are non-issues.

Over the past two decades, more than half the states have passed laws allowing private corporations access to inmate laborers. With rates of pay as little as 50 cents an hour or in some cases $3 a day, companies like TWA, Microsoft, Victoria's Secret, and even Toys R Us have taken advantage of the virtually slave labor. In fact, when it comes to privatization and prison labor, the parallels to American slavery are striking: the majority of the inmates in question are Black or brown-skinned people; in some cases, private prison laborers are accompanied by a guard or overseer; the jobs of free laborers are threatened by prison laborers as their wage significantly undercuts the minimum wage; and the wave of the future seems to suggest that private prisons will hire out laborers in the same way that plantation owners hired out slaves.

The private prison industry is a product of the 1980s and 1990s prison population explosion, but in many ways it is a natural result of globalization. Its rise was a direct response not only to the need for more beds due to high imprisonment rates but also to the free market madness of the 1980s and 1990s that championed privatization—the rise of private industry to meet governmental needs. The privatization of prisons became a reality with our generation. Although it began with privately run halfway houses and juvenile detention centers in the 1960s and 1970s, overcrowded prisons in states like Texas and Tennessee led to a blossoming of private prisons to meet state prison bed needs. Private prisons were initially built after reaching contractual agreements with the states, but the current trend is to build the prison with the hope that customers are imminent.

Privatization of prisons is just another example of globalization's impact on our generation. From drug stores to hardware stores to bookstores to entertainment to heath care to radio and television stations to prisons, mega-corporations have come to dominate our lives. As jobs disappear for the working class and the poor and as inequalities in wealth continue to escalate, what will become of those not working that keeps them cost-effective in a society where the bottom line has come to mean everything? Whether spoken or unspoken, realized or coincidental, prisons have become that answer. Young Blacks are on the front line of this trend.

Opponents of the privatization of prisons often refer to this industry as the "prison industrial complex." However, such a structure has not yet been fully actualized. The leading prison construction and management corporations, including those using prison labor, are effective at lobbying for their interests, but they do not yet dictate public policy concerning prisons and have not lobbied for harsher prison sentences or other laws that would guarantee them a steady stream of clients; neither do the number of inmates engaged as corporate prison laborers or incarcerated in private prisons bear this out. Only 80,000 prison laborers are currently hired out to private companies, and according to private prison industry analysts, only around 100,000 inmates are housed in private prisons, with projected growth to 350,000 by 2004. Given that the total population of those incarcerated in the United States is quickly approaching 2 million, at this point the private sector in prison housing and labor is only scratching the surface.

A major obstacle is labor unions, such as the AFL-CIO, which have spoken out against the ways that prison laborers and non-unionized staffers of private prisons undermine regular workers. Studies are inconclusive as to whether indeed private prisons save money, although industry analysts claim that costs at private prisons are 10–15 percent less than at government-run facilities. In some cases, lawmakers at federal and state levels have given the nod to policies that could eventually make the prison industrial complex a reality. Tennessee lawmakers, for example, have made repeated, though unsuccessful, efforts to turn over part or all of the state prison system to private prison companies.

Resistance to private prisons persists, however. In March 1999, members of a bipartisan congressional committee introduced a bill prohibiting the housing of federal inmates in private facilities. Increasingly, state and federal lawmakers are moving to regulate private prisons. At issue are maximum security inmates (an area that private prison agencies are pursuing) and out-of-state inmates.

At most, what we have today is a foundation for what could become a prison industrial complex in the future. Although the drug war's use of mandatory minimums has proven disastrous for Black youth, it has been ineffective at curbing drug use and trafficking. Because mandatory minimums for drug crimes are overburdening tax dollars and catching more and more young whites in their net, lawmakers may begin to rethink these policies. This in itself would probably end any potential reality of a true prison industrial complex.

In the meantime, the inroads that have been made in privatizing the prison industry have created a profit motive for keeping young Blacks locked up. Despite the inherent problems with the criminal justice system, a lobby has been created that has coffers deep enough to fight for its survival. They have as their allies counties, cities, and towns nationwide who compete for the construction of prisons in their communities. Many are suffering from economic decline, and community leaders realize that prisons can bring jobs to revive communities devastated by the changing economy. With these incentives, the future for hip-hop generationers in the criminal justice system doesn't look like it will change anytime soon.

IMPACT ON THE COMMUNITY

Nearly 50 percent of America's prison population is Black, with hip-hop generationers making up a significant proportion of that population. What will be the long-term effects of this warehousing of such a disproportionate number of young Blacks in the criminal justice system? For starters, consider the following.

1. Prison Culture's Influence on Black Youth Culture. One of the best indicators of the degree to which prison culture has been infused into Black youth culture can be seen in the transformation of Black street gangs from the mid-1970s into the 1980s and 1990s. In the 1970s, arrest and imprisonment of gang members led to organized structures within prisons. Prison gangs inevitably became connected to their street gang counterparts. In fact, many gang members report that they first joined gangs while in prison. (Most cite protection as their motivation.) This phenomenon has also affected what experts call gang migration and the evolution of homegrown gangs that in the 1980s and 1990s began to be reported in hundreds of American cities. As the line between street gangs and prison gangs blur, so do the distinctions between prison culture, street culture, and Black youth culture.

The blurring can be observed in the evolution of hip-hop music. As hip-hop culture became more commercialized in the late 1980s and early 1990s, primarily through the success enjoyed by rap music, aspects of prison culture became more apparent in rap music and Black youth culture, from the use of language and styles of dress to extensive commentary on crime and prison life. With so many Blacks entering and exiting prison this influence is inescapable.

2. Black Families in Transition. The immensely destructive impact that slavery had on the Black family intensified in an age of high imprisonment rates, where hundreds of thousands of young Black men and women with lengthy prison sentences are separated from their families. This arrangement affects relationships between children and their parents, relatives, and friends. Often inmates end up hundreds of miles away from their families, making visitation difficult if not impossible. They lament, even for years after their incarceration has ended, time lost from their children and families that can never be regained. Some mothers struggle to keep incarcerated fathers involved in the lives of their children. Those who opt not to often breed longtime resentment. Families are further stressed by having to rely on a single income and the inability of incarcerated fathers to provide for their children does immeasurable psychological damage in a culture where ideals of manhood are connected to a man's ability to provide for his family.

3. Increased Rift Between Young Black Men and Women. Not to be overlooked is imprisonment's impact on already fragile relationships between young men and women. Interpersonal relationships between men and women are put to the test as partners who aren't incarcerated struggle to fulfill physical, emotional, and financial needs in an incarcerated partner's absence and still maintain the relationship.

4. Rising Rates of AIDS Among Young Blacks.   According to the most recent statistics available from the Centers for Disease Control, by 1999 AIDS was the leading cause of death for Black men and women between the ages of twenty-five and forty-four. The CDC also estimates that at least half of all newly reported HIV infections in the United States occur among those under twenty-five and that most of these young people were infected through sexual activity. Although high rates of AIDS among young Blacks has been widely discussed, researchers have been reluctant to add high incarceration rates of young Blacks to the list of primary contributors. However, given the number of young Blacks in American prisons, such a factor must be considered; it is highly likely that Black men who have sex with other men in prison and then have sex with their wives and girlfriends when they return home may be contributing to increases in HIV and AIDS rates among Black women. In *Lockdown America: Police and Prisons in the Age of Crisis* (Verso, 1999), Christian Parenti details the ways that sex—both forced and consensual—is part of prison life, with transsexual, straight, and gay men forced into submissive sexual roles by stronger men, as well as the degree to which rape is condoned by the prison administration: "A conservative estimate is that roughly 200,000 male inmates in America are raped every year, and many are raped daily. The group Stop Prisoner Rape estimates the real figure to be closer to 290,000, noting that most investigations into the scope of sexual terror in prisons and jails do not count inmates who have sex after pairing off for protection, and usually ignores the much higher rates of rape at juvenile facilities."

5. *Mental Health.* America's prisons are environments where the most basic notions of civilization are routinely abandoned, where women are separated from men, where the strong rule the weak, where gangs abound, and where survival skills are critical. "The experience of being incarcerated is a negative one," says Judy Stanley, director of Accreditation for the National Commission on Correctional Health Care and a clinician with twenty-plus years experience in mental health in corrections. "When individuals aren't solid emotionally, they are going to be damaged by that. Very rarely do individuals come out of prison changed for the better. In most cases there is some psychological wounding."

6. *Criminalized Image of Young Blacks.* In a society that has long associated Blacks with criminal behavior, high imprisonment rates reinforce this association in the collective public mind. "Given their high incarceration rates, they must commit the most crimes," the thinking goes. In the 1980s and 1990s, this association intensified, particularly as it was advanced in the media, and helped to justify the high incarceration rates. According to a 2001 joint study by Berkeley Media Studies and the Justice Policy Institute titled "Off Balance: Youth, Race, and Crime in the News," as homicides decreased 32.9 percent between 1990 and 1998, homicide coverage on

network news increased 473 percent. The study also found that Blacks were too often portrayed as perpetrators and disproportionately as victims, whereas Latinos were nearly invisible in the news media except in crime reports. "People rely on the news media for accurate information," Lori Dorfman, one of the authors of the study, told the Associated Press (April 10, 2001). "When it comes to crime, youth, and people of color, they're getting confusion rather than clarity—part of the story, not the whole story." Unfortunately, young Blacks in popular culture also often link criminality with Blackness. Between pop culture and news media reports, misconceptions continue to define "reality" for an uncritical public. What will the future hold when racial disparities like pay gaps, difficulty in obtaining mortgages, SAT scores, and the like become explainable via incarceration?

7. Decline of Black Political Power.   As many as one-third of all Black men spend time in the criminal justice system. Upon re-entering society, many discover that, among other things, imprisonment has robbed them of their voting rights. Only four states (New Hampshire, Maine, Massachusetts, and Vermont) allow inmates to vote. In fourteen states, a felony conviction equals lifetime disenfranchisement. Most of these states have a process by which voting rights can be restored upon release, but it often involves long waiting periods and is a costly procedure, especially for those who have been out of work for years while serving their sentences. According to a 1999 joint study by Human Rights Watch and the Sentencing Project, 1.4 million or 13 percent of Black men are ineligible to vote because of felony convictions.

Although participation in the mainstream political process by eligible voters is at an all-time low, young Blacks are increasingly testing their potential political power. Groups like A Movement for CHHANGE, AGENDA, and Rock the

Vote's Hip-Hop Coalition conduct voter registration drives targeted at young Blacks. However, high rates of incarceration have haunted these groups' efforts as they seek to organize young Black voters into a viable force in American politics.

8. Reawakened Black Political and Spiritual Consciousness. At the very least, imprisoned young Blacks become more familiar with both political and spiritual ideas while inside America's prisons. Most end up more politicized in prison than they were before entering. The political consciousness that prison life nurtures is educating a whole generation about social inequalities and is adding fuel to a potential powder keg created by continued racial oppression.

At the same time, given the mental and physical strain demanded by prison's survival-at-all-costs culture, most also seek some type of spiritual/religious belief, either mainstream or alternative, such as Islam or Five Percenters, as a means of rationalizing their existence. (These groups, like gangs, provide protection, hence the prison system's tendency to classify some groups of Five Percenters as gangs.) Often in this context, the spiritual and political are connected. As inmates ponder the political implications of the mostly poor, Black, and Latino prison population, religious organizations that help make sense of the Black condition serve a dual purpose. That young people's involvement in the Black church and other religious groups remained on the decline during much of the 1990s as prison rates increased suggests that prison conversions are confined to prison. Whether they return to religious institutions later in life and what impact this may have on this generation and the Black community overall remains to be seen.

Finally, social engineers who endorsed imprisonment as a solution to nonviolent drug crimes neglected to consider what would happen when those terms of imprisonment ended. Within ten to twenty years, many of these 1 million prisoners will re-enter society. Some will be in middle age, many will be dysfunctional, and most will be trying to recapture lost years. Some will try to rekindle old relationships. Many will be even more obsolete as workers in America's mainstream economy than they were when imprisoned. What jobs will exist for them? How will they provide for their families? Where will they find housing? How will society accommodate them? Will psychiatrists be deployed to help these individuals and communities, traumatized by race war, heal? If history is any indication, the onus will fall on existing and already stretched thin Black community institutions. Are we preparing those communities for the task?

Long before phrases like "ethnic cleansing" became popularized by the news media, the idea of race war had been prevalent in American culture. Hostilities between American Blacks and whites, rooted in European imperialism and chattel slavery, have only been tempered by the civil rights era. In the late 1960s and early 1970s, some political activists described the relationship of whites to Blacks in America as one of colonizer to colonized. At that time, some activists referred to those imprisoned as prisoners of war. The idea of America maintaining prisoners of war still persists in activist circles; activists protesting America's sentencing laws and the state of its prisons often use this terminology. The high Black imprisonment rates and the ways those convictions have been secured in the 1980s and 1990s (from legislation to law enforcement and prosecution) reveal the degree to which the war on drugs has terrorized Black communities. Even if the intention of the drug war were not racist, it has taken on overtones of a race war that has pitted the white majority against the Black minority, especially the Black poor. In the final analysis, the war on drugs has materialized into a wave of racial attacks on Black communities and long-term detentions unmatched in the modern era. Those in the eye of the hurricane are young and Black. The Patterson family are but fourteen casualties in a war that has claimed hundreds of thousands of hip-hop generationers. Unfortunately, such a fate has become business as usual for young Blacks at the turn of the century.

Prison culture in the 1980s and 1990s has affected not only the manner in which this generation is perceived but the manner in which many within it perceive themselves. Both perceptions have incalculable implications. Nowhere is this more chilling than in its contribution to the growing rift between young Black men and women.

4

WHERE DID OUR LOVE GO?

The New War of the Sexes

You know I
THUG EM FUCK EM LOVE EM LEAVE EM
CAUSE I DON'T FUCKIN' NEED EM.
—JAY-Z, "BIG PIMPIN'"

IN APRIL 1995, THE BOSTON CHAPTER OF THE NATIONAL Coalition of 100 Black Women sponsored a community forum called "Rap Music: Is it the music of our time?" Toward the end of one of the panel discussions, in which the panelists included a combination of rap artists and hip-hop journalists, a young woman in her late teens approached the open mike in the aisle of the packed auditorium. Seconds earlier, during a very heated question and answer period, several older women in the audience were decrying the mostly male rappers' use of the word "nigga" to address young Black men and "bitch" and other derogatory expressions to describe young Black women. Without pause, the hip-hop generationer explained why it didn't bother her that rappers referred to women as "bitches" and "hos." Setting aside the historical weight of such words, she expressed her ambivalence to this name-calling: "I don't think there's anything wrong with it. Some women act like that and deserve to be checked. I know I'm not a bitch or a ho, so I don't care 'cause I know they ain't talking to me."

It is an argument that has been repeated almost verbatim by countless hip-hop generationers. What sounds to some like far-fetched attempts to defend the indefensible and to others like blatant ignorance points to the divide between young Black men and women in our generation. First, such arguments from hip-hop generationers are attempts to defend our generation, which is often under attack by baby boomers. We've been labeled as slackers, confused, lost, and much worse. Second, the mainstreaming of Black youth culture through hip-hop has made these ideas (like the ones expressed in the Jay-Z lyrics above) more universal among young Blacks. The wide acceptance of this logic reveals a change in definitions, identity, and worldview that sets this generation apart from previous generations when it comes to interpersonal relationships, dating, marriage, sex, love, and gender identity. What are the sources of these new attitudes? What has informed them? Where did our love go for each other and, some might argue, ourselves?

THE GENDER DIVIDE

Some answers to these questions can be found in the first signs that a gender conflict was engulfing our generation. In the mid-1980s, as rap music gained greater visibility and influence due to its financial success and popularity among youth, community and college conferences and forums that explored rap's influence became commonplace. Rap groups like NWA advanced a unique style of in-your-face youth radicalism that would continue in rap well into the next decade. Its underlying themes, born out of the youth rebelliousness of hip-hop-generation-style Black power advanced by Public Enemy, X-Clan, and others, were strongly shaped by the economic changes affecting Black youth. The problem was that the new wave of youth radicalism, dubbed gangsta rap, came with a new theme: the very same contempt that young Black men held for racist policing, high incarceration rates, and limited employment options was also directed at Black women.

Album after album was littered with rap songs referring to Black women as bitches, gold diggers, hos, hoodrats, chickenheads, pigeons, and so on. Music videos with rump shaking, scantily clad young Black women as stage props for rap artists soon became synonymous with rap music. Though dominated by what feminist critic bell hooks called "sexist, misogynist, patriarchal ways of thinking and believing" (*Z Magazine*, February 1994), rap lyrics simultaneously addressed every gender issue imaginable from dating, gender equality, and domestic violence to rape and sexual harassment. Due to its role in shaping a whole generation's worldview, including our ideas about sex, love, friendship, dating, and marriage, rap music is critical to any understanding of the hip-hop generation's gender crisis. More importantly, rap music is one of the few existing arenas where the full range of gender issues facing young Blacks is documented in the voices of Black youth themselves.

Rap music has given young Black males a primary avenue through which to access public space—something that they have long lacked. That Black males' sexist attitudes and gender conflicts have persisted as one of rap's dominant themes for more than a decade suggests the extent to which these issues resonate with young Black men. The very misogynist, antagonistic depictions of young Black women in a music form dominated by young Black males reflect the extent of the tension brewing between young Black men and women.

The beginning of a rift was also apparent among college students. Throughout the 1980s, the fragile state of Black male-female relationships was a recurring topic of discussion among Black college students in forums, at conferences, and in and out of the classroom. Issues such as the effect of sexism, racism, bisexuality, and AIDS on relationships, the difficulty that career-oriented Black women face in finding a mate on equal footing, the influence of American society's patriarchal ways of thinking about Black men and women, the impact of rising imprisonment rates of young Blacks on relationships between young Black men and women, and the need to develop feminist awareness among young Black men and women were all subject to debate. Documenting some of these concerns were dispatches from baby boomers like LaFrancis Rodgers Rose's *Strategies for Resolving Conflicts in Black Male/Female Relationships* (Traces Institute Publications, 1985), Audrey Chapman's *Mansharing: Dilemma or Choice* (William Morrow, 1986), and Delores Aldridge's *Focusing: Black Male-Female Relationships* (Third World Press, 1991). Aldridge's work relied on mid-1980s college students' own commentary to set the tone: "The assignment given to a group of Black freshman enrolled in a college humanities class was, 'write a two-page essay on a topic that is of major interest to you.'" Aldridge shares excerpts from four of the essays with the reader. One female student wrote, "Before I came here [the university], I heard that there were a lot of fine Black men on campus. . . . I've met a lot of Black men and every one that I've dated don't know how to treat a sister. But I've been talking to this white boy who sits next to me in my ECON class. We've been seeing each other for three months. He treats me like a person, like a woman likes to be treated. My mother always said that Black men ain't shit!" Like this student's cutting commentary, all of the other essays reveal a complex range of hip-hop generationer attitudes concerning sex, race, dating, love, and marriage.

In 1990 a little yellow book began gaining wide circulation in Black communities across the country, creating a stir in its wake. The self-published *The Blackman's Guide to Understanding the Blackwoman*, by Shahrazad Ali (a baby boomer), became an overnight bestseller and, according to the author, sold upward of 1 million copies. Although part of the public fascination with *The Blackman's Guide* was driven by the animated, charismatic, take-no-prisoners approach of its author (revealed in author appearances on national television talk shows and at countless community bookstores and cultural centers around the nation), the book's incendiary message was the secret to its success.

The Blackman's Guide nostalgically lauded the self-sacrificing helpmeet woman of yesteryear and condemned the "every woman" of the 1990s. Ali also advised that when confronted by disobedient, loud-mouthed Black women, Black men should check them with "No black eyes, no punching in the breasts or stomach, no stomping, and no upper-cuts," but rather "a sound open-handed slap in the mouth," a controversial perspective, to say the least, in a time that coined the phrase political correctness.

Although Ali was not a hip-hop generationer, the community-wide debate sparked by her book exposed the crux of the gender issue facing the hip-hop generation: we are a generation torn between our modern-ness and the cultural vestiges of the past. Cultural and economic forces like the global economy, e-commerce, extreme individualism, our career fixation, and the feminist revolution all converge to redefine relationships between young Black men and women. Of course, the same issues played themselves out in

American society in general. However, the tensions for hip-hop generationers have been especially intensified because of the socioeconomic disparities (from unemployment to incarceration) young Blacks have faced in contrast to their white counterparts.

The community-wide debate set off by *The Blackman's Guide to Understanding the Blackwoman* was reignited by the 1994 Million Man March, which excluded women. Led by Nation of Islam leader Louis Farrakhan, the march was billed as a day of atonement and as a message to Black men to take charge of their families. Once the organizers of the march set the tone, some all too eager participants carried the torch. Pointed slogans such as "It's time we take charge" and "It's time we had our day" became the battle cry for many. The largest mass gathering in the history of the country, the march was attacked publicly and, more harshly still, privately for its exclusion of women and its male supremacist overtones, but the criticism was mixed. Some women, including many hip-hop generationers, felt it was okay that men gather separately, hence the Million Woman March a year later. Others, especially baby boomers with some hip-hop generationers among them, found it divisive and mobilized against it.

To better understand the hip-hop generation's war of the sexes, consider the impact of feminism and women's rights on our generation. Ours is the first generation to come of age with feminism and women's rights so much a part of mainstream culture that most folks have at least a basic knowledge of these rights—even if they are not yet common practice. The outlawing of sexual harassment, gender discrimination, and sexual improprieties in the workplace is specific to our time. And just as we are the first generation to come of age in an integrated America, we are also the first generation to bear witness throughout our adolescent and young adult years to an America where both sex and sexual orientation have been used as weapons in political warfare. Scandals such as the challenging of Clarence Thomas' nomination to the Supreme Court after Anita Hill's accusations of sexual harassment, Senator Robert Packwood's forced resignation in 1995 after more than two dozen women accused him of groping, grabbing, and kissing them between 1969 and 1990, President Bill Clinton's impeachment in the wake of his inappropriate relationship with then White House intern Monica Lewinsky are all critical to this generation's collective identity. Likewise, issues such as the U.S. military's don't-ask, don't-tell policy, same-sex marriages, and hate crimes against gays have played themselves out in the national theater and helped shape our perspective on equal rights. True, familiarity doesn't translate into across-the-board acceptance. However, it would seem that the hip-hop generation would be the last to accept as their own such passé views as those advocated by *The Blackman's Guide* and implied by the Million Man March's call for Black men to take charge.

Quite the contrary. There seems to be a resurgence among many young Black men of outdated ways of thinking, like keeping women in their place by any means necessary. One small group of young Black men who attended the Million Man March, for example, instead of focusing on the goals of the march itself, was searching out women who did attend and telling them to go home. "This isn't for you. This is for Black men," they said, while attempting to chase the women away. Attitudes like these have helped to spark a brasher brand of feminist radicalism among some women (and rightly so) who have become more militant in their struggle against all things oppressive, including Black men. In a scathing attack on the march and what she saw as its anti-Black-woman agenda, feminist critic Kristal Brent Zook, in the November 12, 1995, issue of the *New York Times Magazine*, wrote:

> It wasn't banishment from the march that was so offensive—after all, black women have certainly convened our share of closed-door assemblies. It was being told to stay home with the children, to be quiet and prepare food for our warrior kings. What infuriated progressive black women was that the rhetoric of protection and atonement was just a seductive mask for old-fashioned sexism. . . . The notion of black authenticity tricks us into equating support for the Million Man March, or O.J. Simpson for that matter, with support for black people, because anything else is considered race treason. Well, many of us have grown tired of such backwoodsman reasoning.

The institutionalization of feminist ideas from the academy to civil rights laws (which came on the heels of the modern women's rights movement and the sexual revolution of the 1970s) has heightened sensitivity to these issues within our generation. At the same time, the persistence of old attitudes about gender roles, rooted deep in American and Black cultures and strongly shaped by popular culture and Judeo-Christian ethics, has helped to breed cynicism between young Black men and women. As the debates over the Million Man March and *The Blackman's Guide* revealed, the distance between these varying perspectives (more enlightened views on gender versus traditional ones) has forged an even greater distance between the sexes. Such disparities raise the question, is there a greater divide between Black men and women of our generation than the generation before us? Or are we simply playing out intellectual battles of the older generation (like the battle waged over the portrayal of Black men in the fiction of Black women writers in the 1980s and 1990s, for example)?

Interestingly, Black women intellectuals of the hip-hop generation have not launched a concerted public attack on sexist Black men (not even rappers) to the extent that the previous generation did. For example, prominent hip-hop generationers were painfully missing from the National Association of Black Women's fight against rap lyrics that denigrate Black women. This left baby boomer C. Delores Tucker, alone in the void, to lead the charge, which in the final analysis drew lines in the sand between generations rather than genders.

Perhaps young Black feminists haven't come out publicly against backward Black male patriarchy and misogyny in our generation because we don't have the same type of gender war going on within our generation. Or perhaps it's because this generation of Black feminist thinkers—although on the whole more aware of gender issues—is not as politicized around gender as the previous generation. The few existing critics seem to span a diverse range of opinions.

In Joan Morgan's *When Chickenheads Come Home to Roost: My Life as a Hip-Hop Feminist* (Simon and Schuster, 1999), one of the most widely read critiques of our relationships to date, the self-described "hip-hop feminist" seems to tone down the antagonism.

On the one hand she pays lip-service to feminist ideas with statements like,

> Acknowledging the rampant sexism in our community, for example, means relinquishing the comforting illusion that black men and women are a unified front. Accepting that black men do not always reciprocate our need to love and protect is a terrifying thing, because it means that we are truly assed out in a world rife with sexism and racism. (p. 55)

On the other hand, in so diligently arguing the ways that hip-hop generation women participate in their own oppression, she downplays the anti-Black woman attitudes of some young Black men and like someone emotionally trapped in an abusive relationship, she rationalizes a way to love them anyway:

> So sista friends, we gotta do what any rational, survivalist-minded person would do after finding herself in a relationship with someone whose pain makes him abusive. We gotta continue to give up the love from a distance that's safe. Emotional distance is a great enabler of unconditional love and support because it allows us to recognize that that attack—the 'bitch, ho' bullshit—isn't personal but part of the illness. (pp.75–76)

In being so overly accommodating to unapologetically sexist young Black men, she suggests that the sexes have moved closer together than ever before. And if the sexes haven't moved closer, Morgan's perception of Black women's feminism of our generation finds sexist, misogynist Black men less offensive.

Others, like Akiba Solomon, politics editor at the hip-hop magazine *The Source: The Magazine of Hip-Hop Music, Culture and Politics,* don't seem as far left as Brent Zook, but neither is she as forgiving as Morgan. Solomon says there's definitely an antagonism. "And we need to open up the dialogue, not pretend the antagonism is not there," she says. "You can see it in music video images, rap and R&B lyrics and in our lack of expectations for each other. It's almost to the point where if you have high expectations, you are seen as a wishful thinker, not someone rooted in reality." Solomon says it bothers her that many young Black women have begun to think of having a long-term relationship as something that belongs in the realm of fantasy rather than something that is normal and to be expected.

All three tendencies are rooted in reality. In many ways the hip-hop generation gender gap is wider, but in other ways it has narrowed. Evidence of lessened tension is the handful of pro-feminist men within our generation who sympathize with the plethora of issues facing Black women and speak out against the antiquated views of their male peers—such as Michael Datcher, author of *Raising Fences: A Black Man's Love Story* (Riverhead Books, 2001) and Kevin Powell, author of *Keepin' It Real: Post MTV Reflections on Race, Sex, and Politics* (Ballantine, 1998). For example, Powell, one of the first writers of our generation with a hip-hop aesthetic to gain national recognition, writes in the May/June 2000 issue of *Ms* magazine ("Confessions of a Recovering Misogynist"):

> Patriarchy, as manifested in hip-hop, is where we can have our version of power within this very oppressive society. Who would want to even consider giving that up? Well, I have, to a large extent, and these days I am a hip-hopper-in-exile. I dress, talk, and walk like a hip-hopper, yet I cannot listen to rap radio or digest music videos without commenting on the pervasive sexism. Moreover, I try to drop seeds, as we say, about sexism, whenever and wherever I can, be it at a community forum or on a college campus. Some men, young and old alike, simply cannot deal with it and walk out. Or there is the nervous shifting in seats, the uneasy comments during the question-and-answer sessions, generally in the form of "Why you gotta pick on the men, man?" I constantly "pick on the men" and myself, because I truly wonder how many men actually listen to the concerns of women. Just as I feel it is whites who

need to be more vociferous about racism in their communities, I feel it is men who need to speak long and loud about sexism among each other.

But in the current climate of bitter warfare, the tension is so great that even those men who try to "get in touch with their feminine side" while pulling our brothers' coats are seen by some women as disingenuous. Their suspicions are rooted in the conflicting perspectives coming from young Black men. Interestingly, such inconsistencies run rampant in hip-hop culture. Consider Tupac Shakur's comments in an interview from prison following his sexual assault conviction:

> When the charge first came up, I hated black women. I felt like I put my life on the line. At the time I made "Keep ya head up," nobody had songs about black women. . . . I felt like it should have been women all over the country talking about, "Tupac couldn't have done that." And people were actually asking me, "Did you do it?" (*Vibe*, April 1995).

Given this damned-if-you-do, damned-if you-don't state of affairs, along with a good deal of young Black men who just don't give a damn, many male hip-hop generationers have adopted the anti-Black woman attitudes espoused on many a rap song.[1] Even rappers like Ja Rule, whose popularity in the

---

[1]I discuss anti-Black and anti-women rap lyrics in greater detail in *The Rap on Gangsta Rap* (Third World Press, 1994). Since that book's release, an enormous body of lyrics has been published that echo these same themes with little variation.

past few years was in part due to songs that celebrate "ghetto love," like "Put It on Me" and "Between Me and You," simultaneously spit rhymes laced with anti-Black-woman venom—even on the same album. In pre–feminist movement years, such attitudes might have been dismissed with the lame defense, "men just don't know any better," but how do you explain such wide-reaching misogynistic beliefs when more progressive thought has worked its way into national culture?

TUPAC AND MIKE TYSON

Nothing better illustrates the complexity of our generation's gender conflict than the 1990s sex crimes involving legendary boxer Mike Tyson and rapper Tupac Shakur. Both cases cut to the core our generation's thoughts about gender. At the time of their trials, Tyson and Shakur were two of the most celebrated heroes of our generation. (Even after Tupac Shakur's death and Tyson's fall from grace within the mainstream, they remain so.) Like many hip-hop generationers, they were outcasts in a society that vilifies Black youth. Each rose to the top against the odds and were living inspirations for many hip-hop generationers. Both in their early twenties at the time of their crimes, Shakur and Tyson were volatile mixtures of the youthful energy, exuberance, arrogance, self-confidence, and at times, foolishness that characterize our generation. If the events leading up to their trials don't portray this, certainly their lives following their convictions do.

Public opinion around each of these cases was steeped in contemporary American ideas about race and sex. More important are the views held by young Blacks that came to the surface as these crises unfolded. How did we react to these incidents? How did they shape us? What do our reactions tell us about our thinking about sexuality, the roles of men and women, and mutual respect for each other's humanity and self-worth in American society in our time?

In July 1991, heavyweight champion Mike Tyson made an appearance at the Miss Black America beauty pageant, one of the many attractions of the 21st Annual Black Expo in Indianapolis, Indiana. There he met eighteen-year-old Desiree Washington, a beauty queen from Coventry, Rhode Island, a pageant contestant and recent high school graduate. On July 18, the two went out for a night on the town. Tyson invited her to "go around and see Indianapolis," Ms. Washington later recalled. At approximately 2 A.M. (now July 19), they returned to Mike Tyson's hotel room at the Canterbury Inn. Tyson later described what followed as heavy petting and then consensual sex. Ms. Washington perceived it otherwise, and two days later, after the pageant ended, she filed rape charges against Mike Tyson. During the two-week trial, she recounted how Tyson "jammed" his fingers into her and performed oral sex on her. "He was laughing like it was a game," she remembered. She went on to describe how he held her down, forced himself inside her, then withdrew and ejaculated. "I told you I wouldn't come inside you," she recalled Tyson saying.

On February 10, 1992, a jury (one-fourth of which was Black) convicted the then twenty-five-year-old Mike Tyson on one count of rape and two counts of criminal deviate conduct. He was sentenced a month later to ten years on each count, but the judge suspended four years and allowed the two six-year sentences to run concurrently. The six-year sentence was also to be followed by four years of probation. Subtracting one day for each day of good behavior, Indiana law required him to serve at least three of the six years. Tyson also received the maximum fine—$10,000 on each count, for a total of $30,000. Tyson served the three years and was released from the Indianapolis Youth Center on March 25, 1995.

While Tyson was still reeling from the blows of this legal boxing match and serving out his sentence, another hip-hop generation icon was in the midst of his own sex crime troubles. On November 19, 1993, Tupac Shakur, twenty-two years old at the time, was arrested in Manhattan on charges of sexual assault. He was later indicted by a grand jury on one count of engaging in "deviate sexual intercourse" by "forcible expulsion," and on another count of subjecting the victim to "sexual contact by forcible compulsion." According to his twenty-year-old accuser (whose name was never released to the media), when she came to Tupac Shakur's hotel suite to see him on November 18, she was assaulted by Tupac and two members of his entourage. She told police that Shakur and one of the men held her down while a third man forced her to perform oral sex. Then, she said, she was forced to do the same to Shakur. Shakur agreed that she did return to his hotel suite, but he claimed that the two of them were alone when "some niggas" came in. "I froze up more than she froze up," Tupac told *Vibe* writer Kevin Powell in an interview from prison (April, 1995). "If she would have said anything, I would have said, 'Hold on. Let me finish.' But I can't say nothing cause she's not saying nothing. . . . How do I look saying 'hold on?' That would be like I'm making her my girl." He said that when the other men came in and began touching her, he got up and walked out of the room.

Shakur and the woman agreed that they had met at Nell's, a Manhattan night club, a week earlier where, according to Shakur, she performed oral sex on him on the dance floor that same night. The young woman insisted that she didn't perform oral sex on the dance floor at the nightclub, and her account of events again differed from Shakur's. "Tupac pulled up his shirt, took my hand, traced it down his chest, and sat it on top of his erect penis," she wrote in a letter to *Vibe* magazine published in the June/July 1995 issue in response to Tupac's earlier *Vibe* interview. "He then kissed me and pushed my head down on his penis, and in a brief three-second encounter, my lips touched the head of his penis. This happened so suddenly that once I realized what he was trying to do, I swiftly brought my head up."

Both agreed that later that night, the woman accompanied Shakur to his hotel room, and they had consensual sex. She returned to Tupac's hotel room a week later on November 18 to see him again when the sexual assault ensued. Prosecutors said that one of Tupac's bodyguard's told the woman that Tupac "liked her so much he decided to share her as a reward for his boys." The woman wrote in the same letter to *Vibe* that she and Tupac were alone in the bedroom when the others entered: "As I started to turn to see who it was, Tupac grabbed my head and told me, 'Don't move.' I looked down at him and he said, 'Don't worry, baby, these are my brothers and they ain't gonna hurt you. We do everything together.' I started to shake my head, 'No, no, Pac, I came here to be with you . . . I don't want to do this.' I started to rise off the bed but he brutally slammed my head down."

A jury of nine women and three men convicted Shakur and road manager Charles Fuller, twenty-three, of felony sexual abuse charges but acquitted them of the more serious sodomy and weapons charges. The following February, Shakur was sentenced to one and a half to four and a half years. Shakur was released on $1.4 million bail (reduced from $3 million) eight months later. The rest of the story for hip-hop generationers is now etched in history as one of the most well-known biographies of our time. But let's stay with this incident and the Tyson rape conviction to consider what they tell us about the gender crisis facing our generation.

1. Black male group loyalty is central to young Black male identity. It's as though America has so vilified young Black men that we've circled the wagons, excluding all others, including Black women. Part of this may be largely the result of the convergence of gang culture, prison culture, and street culture within the new Black youth culture (see Chapter 3). Countless rap lyrics speak of sharing women and placing one's "boys" and/or money above one's significant other. Tupac insisted that had he defended the young woman, it would have seemed to his boys that he was making her his girlfriend. According to his own rationalization, it was more important for him to keep the group from thinking this than to use his power within the group to protect her. Male bonding was foremost in his thoughts. Tupac is not alone. This type of in-group male loyalty has emerged as a cornerstone in young Black male culture. It is an attitude that is especially obvious in today's rap and R&B lyrics, which more than any other one source provides us with the most comprehensive access to what young Black males think about young Black women.

Though intensified in Black youth culture, this mentality of male loyalty is reinforced by society in general, including the older generation of African Americans. As the charges against Tyson unfolded and the case played itself out, many Black male church leaders openly defended Tyson, conducting their own form of damage control and spinning the case as a racist attempt by the system to destroy another prominent Black man. The president of the National Baptist Convention, USA was investigated by the U.S. Attorney General's Office in Indianapolis for offering a bribe of up to $1 million to Washington in exchange for her withdrawal of the rape charges. In Indiana in January 1992, the Reverend Girton of Christ Missionary Baptist Church, along with forty other ministers, rallied in support of Tyson. In Harlem, New York, in June 1995, three months after Tyson was paroled, a group of Black leaders, again mostly Black men, including ministers and politicians, held a parade in Tyson's honor and presented him with a $100,000 check for the Children's Foundation. In short, many Black male leaders, in their Black-male-bonding mode, refused to think beyond entrenched American racism—racism in the charges, racism in the jury, racism in the sentencing. For too many Black male leaders, the issue was about race, not gender. Tyson was being brought down by the white man, and in the process, the line of thinking goes, a Black woman was collaborating with the racist system to bring a Black man down. It is a perspective that has worked its way (either consciously or subconsciously) into the worldview of too many hip-hop generationers' idea of Black manhood.

2. Many hip-hop generation men lack interest in or understanding of feminism.   Even after going through the trial, Tyson was still oblivious to the inherent sexism he espoused in his interaction with Desiree and the problem such a perspective poses for young Black women in general. Instead, to the end Tyson insisted he was innocent. "I didn't hurt anybody," Tyson said in a statement at his sentencing hearing. "Nobody has a black eye or broken ribs. When I'm in the ring, I break their ribs, I break their jaws. To me, that's hurting someone," Tyson said. "I would like to apologize to her, but she's not here." He admitted that his behavior was "crass" and that he did do "something." "I have not raped anyone, attempted to rape anyone, or harmed anyone by any means," he continued. "I'm sorry that Ms. Washington took it personally." Like Tyson, despite our coming of age in an era of feminist awareness, too many hip-hop generation men—blinded by their own egos and culturally entrenched sexist beliefs—fail to grasp the critical issues, and they see little value in becoming educated in feminist issues.

3. The objectification of women has intensified during our lifetime. In Tupac's *Vibe* interview, he describes how two of the men in his entourage gazed at the young woman. He says they "were looking at her like a chicken, like she's, like, food." The objectification of women may not be unique to our generation, or to Black men. However, it has become more chronic among hip-hop generation men. Too many young Black men are open, brash, and adamant in voicing patriarchal and oppressive views toward woman. Not only do they believe these views; they swear and live by them. Again, this trend can be observed in popular culture, but it plays itself out in interpersonal relationships in our communities everyday.

The objectification of women prevails in everything from advertisements to pop culture. In March 2000, the Parents Television Council reported in a study titled "What a Difference a Decade Makes" that sexual content on television tripled and television references to genitalia increased seven times in the decade between 1989 and 1999. Sex is being introduced to young people at a very early age, often unfiltered. The wide visibility of sex in popular culture, often as a selling point, demeans sex and takes it out of context. All of this has certainly contributed to the throw-away mentality that some young Black men have concerning their female peers. Even if Tupac did not "give" the young woman to his friends, as the prosecution claimed, the fact that Tupac left the room, knowing the degree to which his male friends were objectifying her reflects his attitude about women. It is an attitude that is prevalent among hip-hop generationers.

4. The intense focus on materialism in our generation is undermining many relationships.   Henry Kissinger, the former U.S. secretary of state, noted that power is the greatest aphrodisiac. Without the allure of Tyson and Tupac's fortune and fame, perhaps neither woman would have gone to their hotel rooms. The women involved in these two assaults are not alone. An intense focus on materialism is characteristic of our generation (among both men and women) and is a critical variable in the shaping (and, at times, undoing) of our relationships. These dynamics strain relations between young Black men and women. Tales of young Black women pursuing wealthy men are rampant in Black youth culture as in the society at large. Rappers have constructed entire rap careers around some women's willingness to trade sex (with or without love) for "ice," "Cristal," and so on. A telling indication of the wide acceptance of these views among young Black women is the success of rappers Lil' Kim and Foxy Brown (both have sold units in the multimillions) and the many young women who identify with them as role models. Three years after her debut album "HardCore," Lil' Kim told *Interview* magazine (November, 1999) of her fan base, "When I first came out guys were loving me. In my first three months on tour, my shows were packed with men. In the next seven or eight months, the whole front row was women."

5. As much as we are different from our parent's generation, we are similar.   Old sexist attitudes such as "it's the woman's fault" persist within our generation. In both the Mike Tyson and Tupac Shakur cases, the female accusers seemed to be the ones on trial. "If the ultimate issue is one of consent or lack of consent, what woman would have gotten down in the middle of the dance floor, in front of people who she didn't even know, and aggressively performed oral sex on a person that she met for the first time?" Michael

Warren, Shakur's lawyer, asked the media. "Even if she had known him for ages, what type of woman would have done that?" In a request for an appeal in March 1993, Tyson's lawyers claimed that in 1989 Desiree Washington falsely accused high school classmate Wayne Walker of raping her. Similarly, many hip-hop generationers blamed the victims and dismissed the women's charges as attempts to "get money," reflecting the pervasiveness of these attitudes and beliefs within our generation.

6. *When it comes to gender issues, hip-hop generationers are willing to disregard the dark side of their heroes.*   Rap stars like Snoop Dogg and Jay-Z and R&B artists like Sisqo and R. Kelly are embraced by both women and men despite their misogynist attitudes and sexist beliefs. The war of the sexes aside, that Tyson and Tupac continue to be heroes for both men and women of our generation reveals a tendency among hip-hop generationers to divorce their meaningful contributions from their shortcomings and to accept this behavior as business as usual. Likewise it may indicate that many hip-hop generationers, including young Black women, believe that either Pac's and Tyson's accusers were lying or they got what they deserved. Both cases and the hip-hop generation's response to them highlight the fact that despite coming of age in a time of feminist awareness, our generation is not unlike previous generations when it comes to the treatment of women.

The heavy media coverage of both trials further polarized young Black men and women by forcing us to take sides, just as it did with O. J. Simpson, Monica Lewinsky, and others. This type of celebrity journalism has taken on a unique form in our lifetime. Increasingly, such journalism chooses a topic and sets the tone for our day-to-day discussions. The media vilification of Pac and Tyson, hip-hop generation heroes, made young Black men identify with them even more. Many refused to accept any criticism of these icons, especially where it concerned gender issues. For many young Black feminists, on the other hand, these cases renewed their beliefs about the staunch backward thinking of their male peers, further widening the hip-hop generation gender gap.

STICKS AND STONES

Those few hip-hop generationers who have deemed Tupac and Tyson irredeemable misogynists have taken issue with their peers who have supported them. Some young feminists consider women supporters confused, at best, or ignorant about sexual violence, at worst. For many young Black feminists, the support their male peers have given Tyson and Tupac reinforces the overwhelming evidence that many Black men do not like or respect Black women. Increasingly, the feeling is mutual. Although this attitude is not universal among young Blacks, it is so significant a segment of our generation that it has become apparent in our day-to-day interactions. For some, the feeling has crossed the line beyond resentment to hatred.

These feelings are intensified among those in the middle of the age group or those in the primary dating and marriage years (mid-twenties to early thirties). These are the years when many young women (and those men who aren't trying to be playas) feel they should be married or at least in a serious relationship with marriage potential. It is also a time when hip-hop generationers are flexing their muscles in the workplace and coming face to face with their employment options. Of course, resentment has existed in previous generations for similar reasons. Yet in this age of global economics, the new realities carry additional implications. Our generation's focus on our careers and the high value we place on financial success have affected our generation's views on sex, love, and relationships. Hip-hop generationers tend to marry later not because we have abandoned ideas of romantic love or are dissuaded by today's marriage rates but because acquiring wealth and establishing our careers take priority over relationships. The realities of today's information-based economy (from the types of work available to contemporary corporate culture) feed the antagonism between young Black men and women. This antagonism is difficult to measure, yet signs of it are prevalent in Black youth culture. Four issues are prominent enough to warrant further discussion.

The first issue concerns how young African Americans perceive themselves economically and politically. Simply put, Black women resent (or at least feel some anxiety toward) Black men due to the failure of Black men to compete and hence bring the race on equal footing with their white counterparts. Likewise, many young Black men resent (or at least feel some anxiety toward) Black women because of the success they've enjoyed in contrast to the overwhelming failure of Black men. Although racism is often publicly rationalized as the cause of this state of affairs, when it comes down to what we personally want in our partners that same racism remains largely overlooked. This resentment was, in part, why many hip-hop generationers identified with Louis Farrakhan's Million Man March. Too many detractors overlooked this point in criticizing the overwhelming support for the MMM. Yet in a patriarchal, white supremacist culture, few can deny that this is a legitimate concern among today's Black youth. When young Black feminist writer Angela Ards addressed similar concerns in *Ms* magazine in an essay called "Where Is the Love?" (August/September 2001), there was little if any feminist uproar. Ards put it this way:

The gendered racism of the corporate world is such that it's difficult even to meet middle-class, straight black men in the workplace; they seem to threaten the white men who dominate. Consequently, many opt for gigs that are better for the soul than solvency. This economic reality is forcing black men and women to address long-held notions about gender roles that were of dubious merit anyway. But it seems that none of us are adjusting well.

Public in-depth discussion around this whole question of gender roles as they pertain to work, relationships, and race relations has been considered taboo in the larger African American community. Among young African Americans, however, the discussion is becoming painfully open and honest—and a lot more vicious. In short, societal norms equate manhood with financial success but simultaneously leave very little room—given the inadequate education, housing, employment, and health care within Black urban communities—for the majority of Black men to achieve it.

This has become an accepted part of American culture. The racist name-calling that ensued at a Hartford, Connecticut, high school football championship game in 2000 between Black and Latino, urban, and poor Weaver High School and white, suburban, and affluent Darien High School is a clear example of this societal acceptance. As Weaver was routing Darien (running for 582 yards, sacking Darien's quarterback eight times, then going on to win sixty-nine to twenty-six), racial slurs were reportedly exchanged throughout the game. Following a touchdown, a player on the losing team reportedly yelled, "It's okay, in five years you'll be working for me." This belief is rooted in the reality of the unlevel playing field that Black, white, and Latino youth are already familiar with at the high-school level, and it greatly impacts interpersonal relationships, especially as more and more young Black women are doing well all by themselves.

According to a 1997 report by the College Fund (formerly the United Negro College Fund), Black women complete undergraduate and graduate degrees at twice the rate of Black men. Between 1970 and 1996, the number of Black women earning law and medical degrees increased 219 percent compared to 5 percent for Black men. During the same time period, the number of Black men earning master's degrees decreased 10 percent, compared to a 5 percent increase for Black women. Black women also made great strides toward closing the pay gap between themselves and white women in the 1990s. Black males have been less successful at that as well.

According to the U.S. Census for 2000, for every 100 Black women, there are about eighty-five Black men. This figure doesn't factor in Black men who marry outside the race (8 percent of Black men age 25–34) or those who are incarcerated. According to the Justice Department, more Black men 18–25 years old are in prison than in college. Larry Davis, a social psychologist at Washington University and author of *Black and Single*, estimates there are five Black men for every ten Black women if one considers such additional factors as unemployment, disproportionate educational attainment, and Black men who are gay. As Black women become more educated as a group, more are deciding that they don't need to be in a marriage to survive (although single-parent income still puts Black women at an economic disadvantage). Marriage, then, has become an option, not a necessity. And given the rarity of the Black knight in shining armor, so to speak, Black women are increasingly opting out.

"If racism results in thwarted opportunities, then I've felt its reach most in my relationships with black men," Angela Ards writes, considering the state of Black male-female relationships among hip-hop generationers and describing the enduring effect that racism has on her and similarly successful Black women. Further illuminating some of these variables as they influence relationships between young Black men and women, she continues:

> By and large, I've entered any place I had a mind to, attended the schools of my choice, landed the jobs of my ambitions. Sure, I've encountered people with funky attitudes; teachers who ranked my test scores as outstanding "for a minority"; or employers who've hired me under EEOC guidelines and then appeared surprised that I am indeed articulate, accomplished, and skilled. And getting stalked in stores under suspicion of shoplifting seems to be the gauntlet run by black girls everywhere. But the sense that my choices are fewer, chances dimmer, comes mainly because I am a black woman trying to love a black man.

Many young Black women, such as Ards, continue to sympathize with Black men because of the extensive impact of white racism on their state of affairs. However, in a climate where public debate continues to dismiss the legacy of slavery in contemporary America, many have come to view young Black men as losers who too often use white racism as an excuse for their failures in education, employment, business, housing, and financial stability. As young Black women attain success against great odds and as they witness the success of other minorities and immigrants, they question their male peers' continuing failure to measure up—especially as some of the more overt obstacles of America's apartheid have fallen to the wayside. This form of pity further feeds the resentment Black men hold toward Black women. Many young Black women still aspire to enjoy the privileges of womanhood that American societal norms dictate being in a stable relationship with a man should secure, and these attitudes are routinely articulated in Black youth culture. Again Ards:

> My love says it would be easier if his black women friends—even the feminists, including me—weren't secretly yearning for patriarchs, a man who admires a woman who can pay her own way but would never let her. A man who plans the dates, drives the car; pays the tab, if not the bills. Who takes charge.
>
> Sometimes. But rather than a patriarch, I'm looking for a better half, a man who steps up and in. Like many black women, I find myself with nets only as wide as I can stitch them, while others turn to me for backup. I'd like to look to someone else for a change; even if it's just to decide which section of the movie theater to sit in. . . .
>
> But on the real, I fear the sister's being used if she's footing the bill. It's conditioning.

Ards is honest about an attitude shared by many hip-hop generation women: they—feminists included—are mad as hell about this state of affairs, they want it both ways, and unlike older feminists, they are willing to admit it.

Despite the gains women have made, Black men resent Black women for bluntly calling them on their inadequacies. Adding to the tension, many hip-hop generation men resent young Black women because they believe that Black women are not penalized for being Black and therefore have it easier than Black men. Further, the logic goes, Black women don't have the burden of being financially successful to the degree that if they fail, they are no longer considered real women. For a Black man, on the other hand, manhood is dependent on whether he can support his family. If not, socially he is seen as less than a man.

"Of course Black men resent Black women," said one twenty-nine-year-old professional Black woman. "Black men feel that white society is more accepting of Black women and find them to be less threatening than Black men." She related an incident from her college years in the early 1990s at Northwestern University. She and her Black boyfriend (unbeknownst to the employer) interviewed for the same well-paying receptionist job. She got the job, whereas he, equally qualified, was turned down. "Maybe they wanted a woman for the job, maybe they didn't want a male secretary, or maybe they didn't want to have a Black male as the first person that folks associated with the company. We both concluded the latter."

All of this leads to even more tension and resentment as hip-hop generationers, both men and women, publicly and privately, quibble over who has it harder in racist, sexist America—Black women or Black men. In this climate, there is difficulty even in the absence of resentment. Akiba Solomon describes the problem this way: "If they [Black men] don't resent you, they put you on a pedestal—the Black queen thing. Both resentment and being put on a pedestal make having a normal relationship difficult because both lead to unrealistic expectations. When people don't meet them, it causes animosity."

The second issue is the current popularity of strip clubs as entertainment for a growing number of young Black men. By the mid-1990s, according to *Gentlemen's Club*, a trade journal for the strip club industry, there were well over 1,500 strip clubs operating across the country in all but three states and most heavily concentrated in New Jersey, Florida, Texas,

Pennsylvania, and New York. Less than 10 percent of these are upscale, including such extras as fine dining and valet parking. Nevertheless, by the mid-1980s, strip clubs overall had taken a dramatic turn away from the days of seedy backstreet hole-in-the-wall clubs to more trendy nighttime entertainment. The adult entertainment industry estimates that strip clubs are a $3 billion-a-year business. Approximately 10 million men twenty-one to sixty-one years old go to strip clubs from once a year to once a day according to industry analysts. About half of these men are married.

Just as Black youth culture has become more mainstream with the hip-hop generation, many young Blacks have delved deeper into the mainstream in terms of our behavior, beliefs, and concerns. With our generation, what Black and white Americans want and desire has become more generally American than either Black or white. This is a phenomenon that sociologists long attributed to membership in the middle class, but it is a phenomenon that seems to defy class with our generation. And just as the rise of the American strip club industry has consumed young white men from all walks of life, the popularity of the strip club has not gone unnoticed by young Black men. The greater visibility and homage paid to strip clubs in Black popular culture, namely in rap videos and films like Ice Cube's *The Playas Club*, reflect real-life trends. Likewise, the growth of younger Black, single, twenty-something patrons has been observed by topless club owners, bartenders, and patrons themselves. A thirty-something hip-hop enthusiast and frequenter of mostly Black strip joints in the New York City metropolitan area reported that in the past few years, he has observed an increase in the number of young Black men at his clubs of choice: "I remember in 1995–1996 when I first started going to Knockers [a Plainfield, New Jersey, strip club], I was one of the youngest guys there. By 2000, there has been a dramatic shift. Now mostly younger guys—in their early twenties—are the norm and I'm one of the oldest guys out." This assessment has not gone unnoticed by hip-hop generation women—including the dancers themselves, those who see strip clubs as degrading to women, and those who could care less. Both young men and women realize that some men have decided to go to clubs rather than spending money and time dating. Whereas strip clubs were once the domain of married men, bachelor party send-offs, and so-called social misfits, there is now a new breed: those interested in women only as sexual objects.

Some feminist critics attribute the strip club boom to modern economics and the social gains made by women. These gains have created a state of affairs where women need men less; hence men are flocking to a place where they can be catered to by women. Some see themselves as symbolically returning to a place that, in their minds, more closely resembles the old relationship between men and women. However, thirty-three-year-old T. Denean Sharpley-Whiting, co-editor of *Spoils of War: Women of Color, Cultures and Revolutions* and director of the African American Studies and Research Center at Purdue University, says that for young Black men, the dynamics are a little more complex. "Men going out and reliving a bygone era is true to an extent, but that's a very bourgeois, middle-class reading. But even further for Black men it is because they don't enjoy the same access/social gains as white men, that the strip club offers up the opportunity for Black men to exercise control." Sharpley-Whiting suggests that what traditionally has been defined as the madonna/whore complex in the mainstream has been redefined by hip-hop generationers as a "Black queen/hoochie complex." "You may find a few Black women dancing at clubs that cater to white men," she said, "but many Black men who seek out strip clubs that cater to a Black clientele are seeking out a certain type of Black woman stripper—not the white American ideal of woman."

The third issue that illuminates the gender antagonism within the hip-hop generation is the way men and women talk to one another. This is evident not only in our tone, which too often conveys a sense of hostility rather than camaraderie, admiration, or affection, but also in our word choice. The use of the terms "nigga," "bitch," and "ho" by Black men and women to address one another has (regardless of class) permeated our colloquial language. And although defenders insist the "n" word is simply a term of endearment, which is often the case, just as often the context is derogatory. Its usage is so extensive and has become such a mainstay within our generation that it is used by many almost as subconsciously as expressions like "uh." Similar patterns are emerging among many non-Blacks who immerse themselves in hip-hop culture.

Another example of this resentment in the way we talk to one another is found in the mid- to late 1990s expression "chickenhead," a derogatory expression used to describe a woman who—lacking any brains but equipped with lots of deviousness—uses her good looks and sex to gain access to a man's money and accompanying lifestyle. Words like these seem to come out of nowhere, drift into our colloquial usage for a time, and then drift out as effortlessly as they appeared. This does not reduce the damage they do while they hang around.

What about expressions like "baby momma" and "baby daddy"? The terms are used routinely by hip-hop generationers to signify individuals who share a baby together. However, the words simultaneously suggest something about the relationship, usually the absence of the child's other parent. Generally speaking, the term connotes that there is no relationship with the other parent. Rather, the association is with the child. Depending on the usage, the expression can sometimes carry one of the following additional messages: availability because the relationship with the child's other parent is over; bitterness that things didn't work out; or hostility between the parents. It is not, however, used to describe couples who are actively involved in a relationship or who are married with children.

With this definition in mind, baby mommas and baby daddies are a category unique to our generation. This is not to say that having children out of wedlock is unique to our generation. What's unique is this generation's open acceptance of it as the norm. As hip-hop generationers have come of age, the stigma that in previous generations was attached to having children outside of marriage has almost disappeared. This is partly due to the increase in divorce rates, which began among baby boomers in the mid-1960s. Many hip-hop generationers witnessed the divorce of their parents and do not view marriage as a panacea. By 1998, according to the National Center for Health Statistics, the highest concentration of unwed mothers (Black and white) were women in their twenties and thirties. The increasing trend of couples having children outside of marriage is a phenomenon that persists across class lines. Although the stigma has retreated, the expressions "baby momma" and "baby daddy" point to the antagonism brewing between young Black men and women who make these dubious social connections.

The fourth issue important to unmasking the growing contempt young Black men and women hold for each other is child support enforcement laws. The toughest of these laws, intended to hold so-called deadbeat dads financially accountable for their children, have come into existence in our lifetimes. In 1975 the Child Support Program, established under the Social Security Act, required each state to develop a child support program that established paternity, located parents, and determined and collected child support payments. Nine years later, Congress enacted mandatory wage withholdings of child support for absent parents who missed a month or more of payments. The 1984 legislation also required states to create guidelines to determine child support payments. In 1988, the Family Support Act authorized wage withholdings for all new cases and mandated that payment amounts be updated periodically. By 1996, the Personal Responsibility and Work Opportunity Reconciliation Act moved states to a more centralized, automated collection system and allowed states to report "deadbeats" to credit bureaus and to locate parents across state lines. The law also required states to withhold or restrict their drivers', professional, or occupational licenses.

Needless to say, collection remains a problem in a tight economy, especially for unskilled workers. Yet the difficulties such laws pose for unwed fathers are endless. Low-income men struggling to make it in today's economy are forced to choose between their immediate needs and their children's needs, which are often associated with the idea of giving money to their "baby momma." Beyond the legal pressure applied to fathers, resentment may come from the disappointment or anger mothers feel over the disappearance of their child's father or from jealousy over new relationships. Some of these new relationships may involve additional children. "The enemy" becomes more and more nebulous, given all the forces at work. It is much easier to direct frustration at the opposite sex in general. Some of those men angry about the degree to which the child support machine affects their personal lives take their frustration out on other women. Those women who feel they have been betrayed and abandoned by men do the same.

In the past few years, American marriage rates have been at their lowest level since 1958. According to the National

Center for Health Statistics, 8.3 per 1,000 Americans married in 1998. And those who do choose marriage are waiting longer. A study conducted by *Bride* magazine, "Marriage 2000: The State of the Union," reported that in 2000, the average bride's age was twenty-six and the average age for grooms was twenty-eight, compared to the average age in 1960 of twenty for brides and twenty-two for grooms. Add to these statistics the fact that today at least one in two marriages end in divorce. Experts say that for Blacks the odds are even worse. According to a 1998 study by University of Illinois sociologist Shirley Hatchett, two out of three Black marriages end in divorce. Despite these odds, if asked what they want when it comes to relationships, the average hip-hop generationer's response probably wouldn't be very different than the aspirations of previous generations—love, children, a stable home, a good life, and even marriage (although many are choosing alternative arrangements) are still priorities.

Aside from the all-out hostility between the sexes, there are still those who love successfully against the odds. The ability of some relationships (in and outside of marriage) to successfully navigate the treacherous terrain is a commentary on the vitality of Black love. These navigational skills are also a commentary on the social, economic, and political conditions we face, which often make it more convenient to stay together, even as those same forces work to pull us apart.

At the core of the young Boston woman's comments at the start of this chapter is the emergence of a distinctive identity among hip-hop generationers. It is clear, however, that the war between the sexes is related to the dismal economic conditions facing young Blacks in America. If, for example, young Black men were more likely to attend college than enter the nation's criminal justice system, if Black men and women were employed, obtained home mortgages, and earned salaries and promotions at similar rates to their white counterparts, then name-calling, resentment, and hostility between young Black men and women would inevitably diminish.

Less contemplated, but equally important, is the extent to which we could intervene ourselves. If we decided to treat each other with human dignity and respect in all our interactions, how far could we go in curbing tensions that pose one of the greatest threats to Black America today? Unfortunately, as the next chapter's discussion of Black gangster films makes clear, contemporary popular culture too often celebrates and reinforces the crises instead of exploring such questions.

5

YOUNG, DON'T GIVE A FUCK, AND BLACK

Black Gangster Films

> A FUCKED UP CHILDHOOD
> IS WHY THE WAY I AM
> IT'S GOT ME IN A STATE
> WHERE I DON'T GIVE A DAMN . . .
> —MC EIHT, "STREIHT UP MENACE"

ASIDE FROM RAP ARTISTS, FILMS RELEASED BETWEEN 1991 and 2001 that depicted gun-toting, ruthless, violent, predatory Blacks killing other Blacks (dubbed 'hood films by industry insiders) have been the most effective medium for defining and disseminating the new Black youth culture. Yet, there has been very little public discussion of the prevailing definitions this wave of films has given to today's Black youth culture, nor has the impact of these films on an emerging Black youth culture been scrutinized.

Films that fit this description emerged in an atmosphere in which criminalization was the unequivocal public policy solution to any major social problem disproportionately involving Black youth. At the same time, contemporary discussion of race in America, locked in a 1960s-style civil-rights time warp, has failed to consider how young Blacks are affected by unique social forces that have created problems different from those of our parents' generation. Furthermore, whereas previously young Blacks lacked significant access to public space to tell their own stories, this decade was marked by young Blacks gaining more significant visibility and leverage than ever before.

Viewed this way, 'hood films attempted to entertain while defining an emerging lifestyle. Unlike films such as *The Godfather, The Untouchables, Scarface,* or *Goodfellas,* which were by no means attempts to define various ethnic or immigration experiences, these films, by their own admission, attempt to define what it means to be young and Black in America at the dawn of the millennium. Advertisements that promoted these films, in addition to film reviewers, spoke of them as "slice-of-life" portraits of the contemporary everyday young Black experience. Often these films relied on the guidance of young Black directors, the star power of popular rappers turned actors (such as Ice Cube, Ice T, MC Eiht, Tupac, Nas), and hip-hop soundtracks to ensure their success. Defending their art, some filmmakers argued that the films defined what was going on in the lives of today's young Blacks. At times, these films precisely hit the mark. At other times, they mythologized rather than illuminated the new Black youth culture. And it is precisely this misinformation about what it means to be young and Black in the hip-hop generation—advanced by young Blacks themselves through Black popular culture—that has done more to exacerbate the new crises in African American life rather than resolve them.

DEFINING THE NEW BLACK YOUTH CULTURE

Beginning in the late 1980s and continuing well into the 1990s, media and entertainment corporations rediscovered Blackness as a commodity. This marketability was signaled by the heightened commercialization of rap music as well as the mainstream visibility of Black fashion models, entertainers, and athletes. Black films also cashed in. Kicked off by the Black-centered films of independent filmmaker Spike Lee in the mid-1980s, this wave of Black films soon came to be dominated by a range of clown-like to buppie portrayals of Blacks, from *A Rage in Harlem* and *Harlem Nights* to *House Party, Strictly Business,* and others. However, by the early 1990s, the films that proved to be most successful in reaching hip-hop generation consumers were those that took on the heady task of giving a big screen interpretation to the myriad forces shaping today's young Blacks. The 1991 release of *Boyz N the Hood* jump-started the trend. John Singleton's film spoke to something that previously had not been given an on-screen reality for our generation. Here was a coming-of-age film for hip-hop generationers (one that follows the main characters from their 1984 childhood to their 1991 teenage high school years) that began to define the new Black youth culture.

Boyz was the first film to hone in on the idea of the young Black male under siege by the new economic realities that drive the prison and illegal drug industries, resulting in early death, most often by gun violence at the hands of another young Black male. (Singleton fails to explore how young Black women are uniquely affected, however.) Young Blacks are born into a brave new 'hood in which no one, neither society nor even our own parents, are doing enough to bring about meaningful social change. Without intervention, young Blacks circle the wagons and rely on ourselves. Most are reduced to their most basic survival instincts. Because of the conspiracy theory overtones, Singleton's analysis falls short of delving into the reasons for unemployment, inadequate education, and urban economic neglect. He does, however, explore elements like the underground economy and the drug war, paying particular attention to the crack cocaine explosion—critical forces in defining this generation. This includes policing (the recurring helicopters overhead), police brutality, and exposure to horrific events at a very young age (dead bodies, random gunfire, victims of crime, and much more). At the same time, these young Blacks are experiencing the same coming-of-age issues as other American teens, regardless of race or class, urban or suburban—contemplating job options as they enter adulthood, SATs, dating, sex, AIDS, sports, rivalries, and gangs.

This slice of everyday life shaping the new Black youth culture knows few boundaries. Although it affects young Blacks growing up in single-parent, female-headed homes, those living with single fathers or both parents are not immune, and neither is the Black middle class. *Boyz* carefully delves into the intricacies of the Black urban middle class and Black poor and the ways their lives intermingle. At times, this is a struggle between what sociologist Mary Pattillo-McCoy calls "street" behavior and "descent" behavior. Pattillo-McCoy notes in her *Black Picket Fences* that unlike the white middle class, the Black middle class lives in close proximity to the Black poor and hence suffers similar perils. *Boyz*'s Furious Styles (portrayed by Lawrence Fishburne) and his son Tre (Cuba Gooding Jr.) are the sounding board for this juxtaposition. Despite his family's middle-class status, Tre is caught up in the same drama faced by his less fortunate peers. Even though his father's guidance pulls him from the brink (whether in his decisions about sex, career choice, or his responsibility to avenge his friend's murder), we see how close he comes.

Singleton also gives us a realistic portrayal of peer pressure, which flies in the face of the popular claim that anti-intellectualism rules in Black youth culture. In Singleton's world, thugged-out characters like Doughboy and Monster may tease Tre for being smart, for having his father in his life, and for being a little more on the straight and narrow, but they also envy and respect him for it rather than ostracize him. He's as accepted in the crew (which Singleton does a good job of distinguishing from hard-core gang bangers) as anyone else.

Another resounding element of the new Black youth culture that *Boyz* got right was the resilient love and hope that persists in alternatives to traditional family and community structures, despite the ever-present horrors of violent crime, drug addiction, and poverty. Families come together to raise children; parents may not be perfect and at times fit into neat stereotypes (such as welfare mothers), but they hold their families together as best they can. We see community residents chipping in to rescue a crack-addicted neighbor's infant from the street as a car approaches; a mother who wants a better life for her son and does her best preparing him for the transition to college football and all it includes; a mother who allows her teenage son's baby momma to move in, giving the new child and teen parents housing and help with child care; a community that surrounds an ex-con with love upon release from prison instead of vilifying him. Even though this community and these families could certainly do better (and whose couldn't?), these are whole families, making due with what they have and trying to do better.

Last and most important, *Boyz* accurately explored the growing sense of nihilism in Black youth culture. Even though the civil rights movement achieved great progress, even though we came of age during the largest economic expansion in our country's history, even though Black youth are more visible than ever and have become icons of American popular culture, we still remain demonized in American society. Hence, there is a prevailing sense among Black youth that our parents, like American society, have failed us.

You see this nihilism in the eyes of Ricky's attackers in *Boyz*, but you also see a different strain of it in Doughboy's worldview. He's not so much a rebel without a cause as he is doing what he feels he's got to do to survive. He lives the code of the streets, whether it means standing up to a stronger opponent as a child to reclaim his younger brother's football, even though he knows it's a losing cause, or doing prison time, or taking revenge for Ricky's murder—even if it means his own death. He knows there is something about this code that isn't the best course of action. At the same time, his options are limited and he can't find a better way. He needs help navigating life. His family, community, and society have failed him. His father is missing. His mother can't answer his question of "why" she favors his brother. And in the face of his brother's death, he concludes, "I ain't got no brother . . . I ain't got no mother either." And of society's failure to intervene, "Either they don't know, don't show, or don't care about what's going on in the 'hood."

Singleton is clear that nihilism is central to, but not interchangeable with, the new Black youth culture. Films that followed, true to Hollywood bandwagon form, attempted to duplicate *Boyz*'s success in tapping into the Black youth market. For most this meant trying to outgun *Boyz*. In so doing, these films went overboard in portraying outlandish violence and in the process constructed a young Black thug genre, almost Black parodies of white gangster flicks. Over the decade, these films (with few exceptions) portrayed the nihilism of Black youth culture in the form of wanton, bloodthirsty, buck willin' violence for violence sake, substituting it wholesale for the new Black youth culture itself.

NIHILISM UNBOUND

Enter the Hughes brothers. Albert and Allen Hughes' 1993 *Menace II Society* took the on-screen gun violence and homicide to a new level. Even viewers who accepted it as a "slice of life" were shocked by this vicious, brutal violence. The Hughes brothers gave us horrific displays of Black-on-Black youth violence at a time when young violent criminals were being labeled "super-predators" and experts lamented the rise of youth crime, predicting a 20–25 percent increase in the youth population by 2006.

In *Menace II Society*, violent beatings are juxtaposed with scenes of calm and normalcy. Moments before one young Black man viciously pistol whips another, the two, Caine and Chauncy, are enjoying a cordial gathering of family and friends. Likewise, the facial expressions of disgust, anger, and rage that permeate Caine's face—when he ferociously stomps and kicks a young man who says he should take responsibility for fathering a child—are wiped clean when his grandfather intercedes. The merciless beating and stomping incidents are surpassed only by the film's gun violence scenes.

The shooting deaths (the murder of two grocery store owners at the start of the film, the carjacking murder, and the murderous revenge on the carjackers) are accented by the humanization of the victims alongside the cheers and encouragement of cold-hearted killers. Harold's desire to defend his BMW rather than give it up in a carjacking and go "out like a sucker" is contrasted with the egging on of the gunman. "Shoot that nigga," one of his attackers impatiently advise.

Likewise, the scene leading up to the revenge is marked by the discussion that takes place in the car as O Dog, Caine, and Awak look for their adversaries. Caine does not want to kill any innocent bystanding old people or children. O Dog responds, "Man, I'll smoke anybody. I just don't give a fuck. . . . We gonna go ahead and smoke all these mothafuckas. I don't care who the fuck is out there!" They proceed to kill both young men. The first is killed with two shotgun blasts at close range. The second is shot in the back at least ten times and five more times with an automatic weapon pressed to his chest as Awak says to him, "Hey homey, you need some help?" As he falls to the ground, Awak fires five more rounds into his body saying, "Punk ass nigga." Through such calm dialogue in the face of brutal murder, the Hughes brothers give the perception that such cold-hearted violence is routine, a way of life in the new Black youth culture. Unlike Doughboy's reflection in *Boyz* that the revenge doesn't necessarily make him feel any better, the characters in *Menace II Society* never feel any remorse for the lives they have taken.

Mario Van Peebles' 1991 *New Jack City* also portrayed amorality as endemic to the new Black youth culture but spoke more to an East Coast/New York City sensibility than the South Central Los Angeles focus of *Boyz*. *New Jack City* is the story of an illegal drug organization's (the Cash Money Brothers) rise and fall in a Black community in New York City in 1986. And not just the Black poor but also the middle class get with it. Kareem Akbar is a clean-shaven, sharp-dressing college-educated former banker, who rather than earn $800 a week at the bank, earns $8,000 a week with the Cash Money Brothers. Ringleader Nino Brown (portrayed by Wesley Snipes) refers to their get-rich-quick scheme as "the entrepreneurial spirit" and describes their drug dream as the "New American Dream."

The 1980s were marked by an increase in economic wealth among the top 1 percent and a decrease in net wealth for households in the bottom 90 percent. The effects of the global economy on Black communities were in full swing by this time. The decline in the Black community's infrastructure was becoming increasingly apparent. It was a time of drive-by shootings, homelessness, gang wars, and extreme poverty for urban communities. At the same time, it was a period marked by the accumulation of extreme wealth by the corporate elite (characterized by financial crises like the S&L and BCCI scandals). This disparate reality is hinted at in the film with phrases like "You gotta rob to get rich in the Reagan era."

The Cash Money Brothers' plan for success includes taking over the Carter Apartments (a public housing project) under the following operating principle: "If the tenants cooperate, they become loyal customers. If they don't, Beirut: they become live-in hostages." The Cash Money Brothers install computer systems to facilitate the operation, establish a factory for production, and create a "security force" to enforce their will. But first they must eliminate the competition. Of course, this includes the violent gun homicide that has become routine in Black gangster films, from drive-bys and shoot-outs to the public execution of a rival drug dealer, while proclaiming to bystanders: "Now that's how you kill somebody, my brother. You get right up on the muthafucka and 'BOO-YAH'—blow his brains all over the sidewalk in broad daylight."

But *New Jack City*'s most significant contribution to the Black gangster genre was its effectiveness at portraying a world where anything goes. Civilization has been flipped on its head. Children are put in lethal danger by adults; the basic family and community structures are disrupted; there is no love for family, relatives, or extended family; and no one is safe from the violence, disrespect, and chaos. The message comes through loud and clear when a wedding is disrupted by a shoot-out between the CMB and their former bosses. Under fire, Nino grabs a little Black girl, an innocent bystander, and uses her as a shield to protect himself.

New Jack City is also characterized by degrading portrayals of Black women. Women are discussed as less valuable than drugs and money, including endless references to Black women as "bitches," "hos," and "skeezers." Furthermore, abusive and violent language is used indiscriminately to describe all women, including those with whom the leading characters are most intimate. In the world of *New Jack City*, Black men and women are at odds with each other, and the divide between them is filled with hatred, disrespect, distrust, and contempt.

By 1995, *Sugar Hill* took the new level of violence to the extreme of nearly replicating Reconstruction-era lynchings. In Ricky's lynching-style murder—beating, mutilation, burning, and hanging—the contemporary urban Black male takes the place of the hooded Klansman or vigilante. In a further escalation, Ray, the lead character, is shot by his own brother, who attempts to kill Ray's girlfriend Melissa to "save" his brother for himself because "you're all I've got."

As *Menace II Society* ends, Caine narrates, "I had done too much to turn back. I had done too much to go on. I guess in the end it all catches up with you." Black gangster films collectively tell us that it is hopeless to try to escape Black urban America. On the one hand, films like *Menace* say, Black youth are America's outcasts and represent a menace to society. On the other hand, young Blacks' anger and frustration with being outcasts—leading to rebelliousness for rebelliousness' sake—further alienate them. Finally, these films portray police harassment, prison incarceration, violence, and death as the destiny of young Blacks. A very important part of this worldview is the sense of resignation and acceptance of the world as it is. And we are led to believe that this glorified lifestyle of violence, chaos, and mayhem, where Black youth are either irredeemable or dead, is representative of the new Black youth culture.

Nothing was more effective at reinforcing the association between nihilism and the new Black youth culture than the Black gangster films' portrayal of the thugged-out young Black male (who lives and breathes the street) as the prototype for young Black manhood, what the Hughes brothers call in *Menace* "America's nightmare—young, Black, and don't give a fuck." This personality varies little across these films. The most divergent are *Set It Off*'s Cleo (portrayed by Queen Latifah), the female personification of the hip-hop generation Black gangster hero, and Joshua (Bokeem Woodbine) in *Jason's Lyric,* who after taking revenge against his enemies and shooting his brother's girlfriend, takes the young, Black, and don't give a fuck mantra to the ultimate level: he commits suicide, announcing, "I have nothing to live for."

In *Menace*, this new Black male comes in the form of actor Lorenz Tate's extraordinary portrayal of O Dog. Angry, bitter, and tired of negotiating preconceived racist notions, O Dog is a walking time bomb who lives in the moment and doesn't hesitate to defend himself against any perceived slight. This includes shooting a store owner and his wife who assume he's come into their store to steal. He later callously shares the store surveillance video that recorded the murder with friends and boasts about it almost as if it is not real, but fiction. "I'm larger than that nigga Steve Seagal. I'm gonna be a movie star." Following the killing, he is described by the narrator as "the craziest nigga alive." This description presages what is to come. Rather than presenting a mythical challenge to America, such personalities in Black gangster films tend to self-destruct, are apolitical, and pose a threat to no one except their own community.

Such is the case of Bishop (portrayed by Tupac Shakur) in Earnest Dickerson's *Juice*. Bishop, a high-school-aged youth, is so fascinated with materialism and power that it causes his self-destruction. He describes his thirst for power, juice, which he believes can be secured and maintained only through violence, this way: "If you want juice, you got to throw down, stand up, and die for that shit . . . If you want some juice, get the ground beneath your feet and go out in a blaze if you have to . . . You gotta take them out anytime you want to. Otherwise, you ain't shit." In the process of living by these guiding principles, he, like nearly every other "hero" of Black gangster films, destroys many of those around him.

BEYOND NIHILISM

Although the nihilism in Black youth culture is the most significant common thread that connects Black gangster films, these films have accurately depicted other elements of the new Black youth culture. *Jason's Lyric* gives us an example of Black love surviving against the odds. *Juice* unmasked violence as an aberration rather than an inherent characteristic of Black male youth. *New Jack City*, in which the criminal lifestyle is presented not as a moral question but as a means to an end, reveals that for many Black youth, money is the only way out of our generation's poverty and outsider status. *Jason's Lyric,* set in the rural/urban serenity of Houston, illustrates that the new Black youth culture permeates Black communities, regardless of geographical setting. Elements like these are often cited as evidence that Black gangster films—despite amplifying the nihilism in Black youth culture—have to some degree accurately described our generation's experiences.

Aside from the nihilism that dominates these films, this wave of like films are bound by one other unifying theme: an attempt to explain the generation gap. Black gangster films are infused with the question, how is it that the hip-hop generation is so different from our parents' generation?

Resolving the hip-hop generation's confusion about the extent to which our own reality—from life advantages to disadvantages, for better or worse—has evolved out of our parents' experience is central to this inquiry. For most of our lives, we've been hit over the head with the civil rights gains as the monumental achievement of our parents' generation, but it is evident to us that those gains haven't secured our inalienable rights. Black gangster films attempt to answer the question, how exactly did our generation's worldview evolve out of our parents' generation? And these films take on this question with all the accompanying cynicism, disdain, and anger that many hip-hop generationers hold for an older generation that in many ways, we believe, has failed us.

Sometimes this inquiry comes in the form of a new generation that has peeped the failure of the civil rights and Black power movements and hence has abandoned the Black cultural tradition of social activism. From this viewpoint, being true to the new Black youth culture requires our generation to ridicule any remnants of Black consciousness and/or community-centered activism as outdated and out of touch with the new realities. Shareef is the vehicle for such commentary in *Menace II Society*. When we first meet Shareef, he's described as an "ex-knucklehead turned Muslim." Prior to this introduction, Shareef is sitting on a beer-filled cooler to "keep you fools from drinking this poison." Caine completely dismisses this thought. "Man you better get your Salakum Salaam ass off that box and pass me a motherfuckin' brew." Caine continues as narrator, "He was so happy to be learning something he liked, he kept coming at us with it." Caine further instructs us, "He thought Allah could save Black people. Yeah right." Historical Black values, in this case spirituality, are presented as played out and odd, hence, Shareef is ridiculed practically every time his words reflect his developing political and spiritual consciousness. Shareef's death at the end of the film is clearly contrasted against the backdrop of O Dog's life, suggesting that Shareef's lofty, romantic, and nostalgic politics and spirituality could not save him. According to the film's logic, O Dog's lifestyle and worldview keeps him alive, while Shareef's worldview has no place in the rough, tough, and dangerous 'hood. Ultimately, the film asks, who possesses the lifesaving knowledge?

Another feature that Black gangster films use to question the connection or separation between the generations is the suggestion that the new jack Black gangster's arrival is an immaculate conception. Ours is a generation that has birthed itself. In this view, the new Black youth culture is a complete breakaway culture that is an outgrowth of the conditions of our time rather than a cultural continuum. In this line of thinking, the old arguments of integration versus separation no longer apply. In fact, most Black gangster films pretend that the historic struggle between integration and separation is resolved in our generation. The answer is the young, Black, don't give a fuck hip-hop generationer, a new millennium version of the old one's "bad nigger." In this context, only street culture (hustlers, pimps, playas, bitches, and hos) evolved, not the social activist element.

This does not mean there isn't nostalgia for 1970s street culture. But it is a nostalgia that allows hip-hop generationers to distance ourselves, while pretending to embrace a generation that many of us feel a great deal of animosity for. For example, *Menace* and *Sugar Hill* show us an older generation that we've evolved from—not only as direct offspring but even in our adherence to our parents' code of the streets. *Menace*'s O Dog is the son of a 1970s version of the blood-thirsty, nothing-to-lose, new young Black male. *Sugar Hill*'s drug-dealing lead characters are sons of drug addicts. The suggestion is that this criminal-minded street culture is transmitted genetically from one generation to the next. Such films emerged at the same time as the supposedly-scientific theories of Charles Murray and Richard Herrnstein's *The Bell Curve* and alongside public policy that suggested that welfare, crime, and violence were Black problems, but also genetic ones. In *Sugar Hill,* this idea is established by suggesting a connection between the lead characters' drug-addicted parents and their own involvement in the drug game. They transcend their parents symbolically; Roemello embraces his father while he and his brother emerge as drug dealers par excellence, and in true Oedipal fashion, his brother Ray murders their father in an attempt to "put him out of his misery."

Hip-hop generationers, this line of thinking goes, were born into the game. But more so, we have out-pimped the original pimps, out-gangstered the original gangstas, macks, playas, bitches, and hos. At the forefront of advancing this school of thought are the Hughes brothers. Their 2000 pseudo-documentary, *American Pimp,* is more a cut-and-paste journey into selective memory of what we've inherited from our parents' generation than it is a look at a social phenomenon. Like the fictitious gangster films, the Hughes brothers lean on a hip-hop-heavy soundtrack—laced with R&B classics to strengthen this association. In addition to this backdrop, we get commentary from young twenty- and thirty-something up-and-coming pimps (including commentary from the notable rapper Too-Short and more obscure rappers), as well as old-school pimps like Filmore Slim and Bishop Don Magic Wand. With representation from most regions of the country (East Coast, West Coast, Midwest, and Dirty South), the message is that this new Black youth culture—pimping included—is national in scope. This focus on pimping, particularly its 1970s manifestation, as a phenomenon to be emulated in the present, especially as the vernacular of pimps, playas, bitches, and hos has gained currency in contemporary rap music and hence among young Blacks, is hardly coincidental. However, it adds to the Black gangster films' mythology of a new Black youth culture as more of an outgrowth of the street culture of our parents' generation—diminishing our parents' more praiseworthy achievements and our own. The message here is, they left nothing better and we aspire to nothing more meaningful.

American Pimp relies on connecting the previous generation of pimps to the present one mostly in the form of advice from old heads to new jacks, idolization of pimp legends, contrasting 1970s playas balls to contemporary ones, throwing in images of blaxploitation films for good measure (further distorting the historical record), and highlighting how a new generation is picking up the torch and keeping the tradition alive. To their credit, the Hughes brothers do include commentary (however limited) on the downside of pimping and ho-ing for men and women. Yet this doesn't diminish the celebration of pimping as part of what it means to be Black then and now.

All of this revisionist history buckles under the weight of the nihilism that permeates Black gangster films. One possible exception is the message that Hype Williams gives us in *Belly*. Williams makes it clear that our evolution comes out of both street culture and the socially responsible element. In *Belly*, both get morphed along with the new realities of our time to give us a redemptive new young Black man and woman who supersede the young, Black, and don't-give-a-fuck persona by respecting the power and limitations of both. The kill-or-be-killed mentality of the street is real life. The ability to navigate it is essential in a survival-of-the-fittest world. Yet Williams makes it clear that true survival requires elevation out of the muck and mire of senseless murder and dead-end living.

Like other gangster film heroes, the lead characters Tommy and Sincere (portrayed by rappers DMX and Nas, respectively) initially view getting money, by any means, as the solution. "You think another motherfucker know what you need to do?" Tommy barks at Sincere in a discussion about a book Sincere recently read that leads him to question his purpose in life. "Ain't no purpose. We born to fuckin' die. In the meantime, get money." But over the course of the film, Tommy goes from prototypical, thugged out, ruthless killer to new Black man redeemed, or at least someone who is ready to "make things right."

In Sincere, Williams gives us another recurring character type in Black gangster films: the conscientious, in-it-but-not-of-it, street-savvy brother aspiring to do the right thing. Transcending characters like *Boyz*'s Doughboy, however, Sincere not only recognizes that something is wrong with the hand young Blacks have been dealt, but seeks a way to intervene—at least on behalf of himself and those he can touch. "I don't have to play the part of the whole movement," he says to Tommy as both begin to turn the corner, "but if you raise your family right, it will be all right."

Finally, in the romance between Sincere and T (portrayed by R&B singer T-Boz), Williams gives us a nonviolent, loving relationship working against the odds. Rather than recast what UCLA assistant professor of history Scot Brown calls the "confused Black woman at the crossroads," the whining Black woman who wants to leave her criminal companion but is caught between her moral center and her strong feeling for the male outlaw, Williams gives us a new Black woman in T. This moral center in *New Jack City* leads Ms. Thomas to testify against Nino to help law enforcers bring him to justice and in *Menace II Society* causes Ronnie to continue her involvement with Caine even though he won't let go of the street life. T transcends both these characters as she commits herself to escaping the decadent, destructive, and irredeemable chaos with her family intact and encourages Sincere to do the same.

As Tommy, Sincere, and T come full circle (Tommy to accept the spiritual and political teachings of the film's spiritual lead, Reverend Savior, and Sincere and T to follow their dream of getting out the 'hood and moving to the motherland—subject for another essay), Williams has given us an alternative definition of the new Black youth culture. Young Blacks seek a way out of the madness, and even the most extreme outlaw types (in this case Tommy) are open to the Black traditional message of social responsibility. "Help me to stop the slaughter of our children. Help me to stop the dishonor of our greatest resource, the Black woman. Help me to end the destruction of young minds through the use of drugs and alcohol. Help me to build a population of young thinkers, people who will create change through thoughtfulness and spirituality." Rather than end with the nihilistic message of previous Black gangster films—that our generation lacks self-determination, and personal responsibility is not part of our generation's identity—*Belly* embraces a more redemptive theme. In doing so, *Belly* more honestly and courageously bridges the gap between our parents' generation and our own.

The financial success of Black gangster films points, in part, to the failure of Black intellectuals to make sense of the critical changes in African American life. Filling the void, over a decade, are Black gangster films. The degree to which the fantasy of film interfaces with reality in the public imagination, especially in the imagination of the younger generation for whom such image-induced definitions are central to our identity, can no longer be ignored. For young Blacks grappling with questions on their own—some living close to the battlefield and others in the thick of it—popular culture, including films like these, rather than societal institutions, have provided the answers—often wrong-headed ones.

For better or for worse, Black gangster films have helped to shape a generation's consciousness. Where they accurately depict the new Black youth culture, they have helped to reinforce the rap messages that solidified our generation's youth culture. Where they are wrong, the misinformation—given the power and pervasiveness of visual images in our information age—contributes to the crises in African American culture.

More often than not, these films drown out a precise definition of the new Black youth culture—particularly when there are shreds of truth lingering in each. The elements glorified and idolized in Black gangster films, then, add fuel to the fires of gender, generational, and racial divisions. The depiction of pimping, macking, playas, bitches, and hos as integral aspects of Black youth culture breeds even greater resentment between young Black men and women. Pretending that conflicts don't exist between the generations, advancing nihilism as Black youth culture, and denying the existence of a continuing Black tradition of social responsibility in our generation only help to reinforce the antagonism between young and old, especially older middle-class Blacks who tend to view the new Black youth culture as ghetto culture. The crises of unemployment and prison incarceration are both deepened as representations in Black gangster films encourage young Blacks to continue the cycle of criminality as if it were part of our identity. Such misinformation provides justification for social policy and legislation that criminalizes Black youth, as society increasingly looks to the mythology of film as a substitute for hard facts. The extent to which the worldwide distribution and consumption of these images in a global economy have contributed to the national and international backlash against Black youth is impossible to measure.

What is most often missing from Black gangster films and popular discussions of Black youth are those who find possibility within the hopelessness. This is what makes rappers like Jay-Z and b-ballers like Allen Iverson so messiah-like to today's Black youth. Hip-hop generationers identify with not only their success but where they came from, who they continue to be, *and* the success. This adoration goes beyond simple fascination with or worship of pop culture icons. These hip-hop generation icons have been effective at what Mike Tyson called, in describing the secret to his success, "turn [ing] the fear into fire."

These icons may stand out in terms of visibility, but they are not alone. Other examples of hip-hop generationers turning the fear into fire are found among our generation's activist and political thinkers, who probably better than anyone else have bridged the gap between our parent's generation and our own—and in the process have begun the daunting task of constructing workable solutions.

Part TWO

CONFRONTING THE CRISES IN AFRICAN AMERICAN CULTURE

6

ACTIVISM IN THE HIP-HOP GENERATION

Redefining Social Responsibility

IT'S NOT IN THE OLDER GENERATION'S BEST INTEREST TO CULTIVATE A HIP-HOP GENERATION OF LEADERS. OLD HEADS IN POWER ARE THREATENED BY THE POWER OF HIP-HOP. GIVEN THE WAYS WE CONTROL THE MARKETPLACE AND DOMINATE POP CULTURE, THEY REALIZE THAT IF WE EVER TURN THAT ENERGY ON TO COMMUNITY AND POLITICAL ACTIVISM, THEN IT'S ALL OVER FOR THEM.
—LISA SULLIVAN, FOUNDER AND PRESIDENT OF LISTEN, INC.

IN EARLY MAY 1994, ON THE EVE OF NEWARK'S MAYORAL election, twenty-five-year-old Ras Baraka, son of the famed 1960s activist-poet Amiri Baraka and a leading challenger in the race, was asked why he was staying in Newark given all the problems facing the city. "I love my community, and I'd rather stay here and fight for what we should have," he told the *New York Times*. "I think it's a cop-out to run away. I grew up here fighting for things that didn't matter. I might as well fight now for something that makes a lot of difference." Although Baraka lost the mayoral bid and a subsequent run for city councilman-at-large four years later, as a community organizer, the Newark native and eighth-grade teacher continues to pose a real threat to business as usual in Newark.

While New Jersey's largest city is being staked out by Ras Baraka and other hip-hop generationers like thirty-one-year-old Councilman Cory Booker, Midwestern Black strongholds like Chicago are also feeling the presence of the hip-hop generation. In 1995, Illinois Congressman Mel Reynolds fell from glory after he was charged with having a sexual relationship with a teenage girl. His conviction left his congressional seat empty, and Chicago's Democratic machine, under the watchful eye of Mayor Richard M. Daley, endorsed Emil Jones Jr., the Illinois Senate Democratic leader. But the old guard had to give way to the hip-hop generation, as newcomer Jesse Jackson Jr., son of the civil rights firebrand Reverend Jesse Jackson, won the seat in a landslide victory. Now in his third term, the thirty-five-year-old has served as congressman for the 2nd District of Illinois (which includes the far South Side and south suburbs) ever since. "Ninety percent of the racial debate is really about economics," says Jesse Jackson Jr., who along with other hip-hop generationers are restructuring the discussion of America's race problem, among other issues, for our time. "If we frame the discussion in terms of growth, jobs, the economy, we can move beyond the racial battleground."

Undoubtedly, part of the status that Ras Baraka and Jesse Jackson Jr. have achieved as activists/politicians comes from their familial connections. Yet a significant aspect of their strength and popularity is more about their generation than their heredity. This generation represents a new age in

Black America's political activism. Baraka's and Jackson's comments, cited above, reflect both a new level of political sophistication for Black politicians and a new political reality. They, like other hip-hop generation activists, are ever mindful of the previous generation's grassroots efforts and mainstream civil rights success and periodically bring that weight to bear. But they aren't locked exclusively into an old-school civil rights establishment agenda. This combination has helped hip-hop generation activists and politicians forge a unique brand of activism and politicking, with an eye on both the past and the future. It's a connective thread that runs throughout the activism of this generation.

ACTIVISM AND THE HIP-HOP GENERATION

The hip-hop generation's brand of activism has its own intricacies. To begin with, it is distinguished by the fact that we are the first generation to come of age in an America that has ended legal racial segregation. We are the first generation of African Americans to enjoy the fruits of the civil rights and Black power movements. Voting rights, affirmative action, the rise of Black elected officials, and social programs benefiting the poor have all been part of life as we know it. At the same time, we've witnessed the steady erosion of the euphoria of racial integration and in some cases civil rights gains themselves. Due to the nature of the America we've grown up in, we've developed a different sense of urgency rooted in what we've lost in a mere generation—what some critics have deemed the reversal of civil rights gains, such as welfare reform and the decline of affirmative action—as well as in new attacks targeting Black youth like police brutality, anti-youth legislation, and the incarceration of hundreds of thousands of hip-hop generationers. We don't mythologize the social gains of the 1950s, 1960s, and 1970s because having experienced the benefits of these gains firsthand we know they weren't panaceas. At the same time, we do romanticize them. They, along with other so-called civil rights gains, have been institutionalized in the present as part of America's glorious history. They stand in our collective memory as historical wrongs corrected. Nevertheless, hip-hop generationers realize that no matter how groundbreaking the civil rights movement was, unfinished business remains.

As children of the civil rights generation, hip-hop generation activists belong to a generation of privilege, privileges afforded us by the civil rights gains. And thanks to the civil rights movement, we've had more time to think through the issues without having to test theory in the fire of an intense and confrontational day-to-day struggle. Race issues in our time, aside from those measured by statistics like racial profiling, imprisonment rates, and housing discrimination, are more covert. Our activists are often better educated and better informed, more luxuries afforded us by the previous generation's victories. All of the above circumstances have shaped our commitment to activism, have influenced our waning interest at times, and have affected our inability to turn up the heat even on issues that concern us most.

Inasmuch as we are indebted to civil rights/Black power activism, our generation's lack of a mass political movement has also influenced our activism. The previous generation had the luxury (if you want to call it that) of a broad-based movement. In a climate that screamed for change, youth movements across race, class, gender, and ethnicity were part of the culture. Anti-war activism, the African independence explosion, political revolutions in Central America and Asia were all underway. In that time of national political movements and youth radicalism, fighting the power was a given, and the lines of battle were more clearly drawn— mostly in Black and white. The 1950s and 1960s brought many changes in law, and the early 1970s ushered in an age of Black elected officials, but the 1980s and 1990s were void of any significant movement around which young Blacks could organize at the national level. For us, in part due to the previous generation's victories, today's "enemy" is not simply white supremacy or capitalism. White supremacy is a less likely target at a time when lynchings aren't commonplace (in the traditional sense) and when Blacks can vote and are not required by law to sit in the back of the bus. To deem capitalism the enemy when financial success and the righteousness of the free market have become synonymous with patriotism is hardly popular.

Although we lack a broad national movement, we are not without smaller-scale activist movements. Police brutality, mandatory minimum sentencing, and the death penalty are issues that began picking up national momentum and popularity with Black youth and galvanizing activist efforts by the end of the 1990s. As the issues have diversified with our generation, young activists are more likely to focus on a particular issue. Some hip-hop generation activists tend to work in isolation. Nonetheless, our generation focuses on a wide range of issues: racial profiling, environmental justice, electoral politics, youth issues, parenting, globalization. For us, these are many heads to the same monster.

Another characteristic of the hip-hop generation's activism is that the opposing traditions within historical Black political and intellectual thought, such as revolutionary versus reformist, radical versus accommodationist, and nationalist versus integrationist, have moderated from their polar extremes. The evolution of Black political thought from the Black power generation to the hip-hop generation has blurred the boundaries of the traditional political perspectives. At times the fusion of opposites has been so dramatic that it is difficult on the surface to distinguish them. In essence, the mainstream has been radicalized and the radical has moved farther into the mainstream. This is true of activists like Ras Baraka, who voice what would historically be characterized as a revolutionary/nationalist perspective and those like Jesse Jackson Jr., who historically is more in synch with the reformist tradition.

This blurring of political boundaries can be explained by the pragmatic attitudes held by hip-hop generationers. We accept how truly American we are—if for no other reason than African Americans' long tenure in and contributions to America. Even those wrapped in the most radical political perspective feel entitled to their piece of the American pie. At the same time, even the most reformist/integrationist-oriented hip-hop generationer recognizes the disparate treatment of African Americans and realizes that change is necessary.

As the political spectrum within African American political thought among hip-hop generationers has narrowed in terms of the historic tendencies, it has also become more diverse. The new generation is characterized by the rise of conservatism and increased tolerance of alternative political views. Hip-hop generationers are not as predictable in their political or ideological persuasions, due in part to many young Blacks' dissatisfaction with the Democratic Party; hence young Black conservatives are no longer excommunicated the way our liberal parents ostracized Black conservatives of their generation. The new wave of young Black conservatives, some of whom identify as Independents and some of whom identify as Republicans or at least sympathize with Republican Party concerns, has gained ground in this generation. A 1999 Gallop Poll reported that 44 percent of Blacks eighteen to thirty-four years old identified themselves as Independents—exceptional in a traditionally Democratic demographic. Our generation seems to be more accepting of this as hip-hop-influenced conservatives like Oakland NAACP president Shannon Reeves, Stepson Records CEO and political activist Bill Stepheney, former speechwriter for Newt Gingrich and PolitcallyBlack.com founder Charles Ellison, and *New York Post* columnist Robert George enjoy wide popularity among their peers, regardless of party affiliation.

"Many young Black conservatives have a self-help, nationalist message and are looking at current political situations from a Black perspective," explained thirty-one-year-old political commentator Lee Hubbard. "Many also got into activism during Jesse Jackson's campaigns in 1984 and 1988 and were energized by Jesse's talk of forming a third party, but became disillusioned when there was no follow-through and Jesse went full-fledged Democrat. A lot of the issues like less government, less welfare, and anti-abortion sentiment resonate with core sectors of the Black community, so it shouldn't be surprising that you see young Blacks jumping on conservative politics."

Older, Black-centered, and Afrocentric activists have long shunned this right-leaning element, but it represents a long tradition in Black American political activism and thought. The hip-hop generation is more apt to embrace alternative political perspectives and is not as rigidly confined to the political boundaries that often undermine the older generation's long-term goals.

CAREERS OVER ACTIVISM

The hip-hop generation is often miscast as a generation lacking political activists. Although there are several reasons for this misconception, the most evident one centers on the all-pervasive popular culture, where young Blacks, mostly professional entertainers and athletes, gain wide visibility by association with corporate products. As activists' causes and concerns generally run counter to corporate interests, to-day's young Black professional athletes maintain a code of silence when it comes to political issues. Michael Jordan's si-lence on the issue of Nike's low-wage factories and high-priced shoes bears this out. Those who challenge this code, such as Mahmoud Abdul Rauf's refusal in 1996 to salute the American flag and stand for the national anthem at NBA game-time, suffer serious consequences.

Among accomplished actors and musicians, it has be-come sexy to periodically champion a cause—albeit not one too radical and certainly not too early in one's career. Vet-eran actor Danny Glover, an outspoken anti–death penalty activist who has provided visible and financial support to political concerns like the Washington, D.C.–based foreign policy lobby group TransAfrica, is a rare figure in Black Hol-lywood for any age group. Few hard-core activists would consider Glover radical, yet his outspokenness, given the visibility he enjoys, is quite rare for today's Hollywood. To date, no actor of the hip-hop generation has matched Glover's political courage.

Arsenio Hall, a baby boomer, serves as a point of refer-ence. Hall had one of the hottest late night shows in town until he went against the grain in inviting Minister Louis Farrakhan to appear as his guest in March 1994. Two months later, the show was canceled, with network executives citing low ratings due to the return of David Letterman to CBS. And when the Reverend Jesse Jackson staged a protest of the Oscars in 1996 due to the Academy Awards' repeated failure to acknowledge Black talent, few actors or actresses sup-ported him. (That year 165 of 166 nominations went to whites.) The message is clear to today's would-be and estab-lished professional Black athletes and entertainers: there are no activists here. It is a message that begins within the pro-fession but along the way gets transmitted to legions of fans and supporters. Its pervasiveness is a landmark, however inglorious, of this generation.

Influence of popular culture aside, the gains of the civil rights/Black power generation were so large and transformative that that historic period has come to define what activism is. The civil rights movement is extensively debated and taught in our schools and is commemorated during holidays and observances like Martin Luther King Jr. Day and Black History Month, year after year. Future movements are impossible to conceive and activism that produced significant social gains prior to the 1950s and 1960s has been all but forgotten. Current forms of struggle that go outside the civil rights box are ignored or deemed meaningless.

It is true that compared to our parents generation, we lack a sustained political movement (our activism, in fact, seems watered down by comparison). This may also explain why activism is less attractive to many of us. One of the obstacles to activism in this generation is one that worked to disrupt the civil rights and Black power movements. The setbacks that the movements suffered at the hands of local police action and the FBI's COINTELPRO strategy (including J. Edgar Hoover's mission to stop the rise of a "Black messiah") are now legendary. The attacks on Black activists—including shoot-outs between police and activist groups like the Black Panthers, police-instigated battles between various activist camps (such as the Black Panthers and US Organization), the assassinations of Dr. Martin Luther King Jr., Medgar Evers, Malcolm X, and others, and the imprisonment, often unjust, of activists like Geronimo Ji Jaga, Assata Shakur, and Dhoruba bin Wahad in the 1960s and 1970s suppressed activists during that time, but have discouraged this generation of activists as well. Those physical and psychological blows—alongside today's even more sophisticated and often blatantly racially

unjust criminal justice, policing, and incarceration systems—have had one of the greatest silencing effects on today's hip-hop generation activists and would-be activists.

The deterrence to activism in our generation may have
also inadvertently encouraged this generation to choose career over activism. Few hip-hop generationers can resist the
omnipresent consumer culture. Add to this the complexities
of the national economy we've witnessed in the 1980s and
1990s. Although the recent economic expansion was historic,
study after study has shown that its gains did not make life
better for most people. The lifestyle enjoyed by working-
class people in the 1960s and 1970s is a dream unfulfilled for
most working-class folks today. Consistent with these economic challenges, pursuing financial security through careers in the mainstream economy and, at times, the underground economy (among the poor and middle class) have
taken priority over activists' concerns for most hip-hop generationers.[1]

ACTIVISM VERSUS ACTIVIST-MINDED

What follows are profiles of some of our generation's leading activists. It's important to make specific references here
because activists in our generation receive so little attention;
far too few people, in either the older or younger genera-

---

[1]This is not meant to dismiss those hip-hop generationers who use their careers as a way of strengthening their activism. Many of us believe that we
do "the people" or "the cause" no good if we can't meet our own basic
needs. We realize that a large segment of our people are drawn to financial
success and wealth, not necessarily those who have the best "rap," so to
speak. Likewise, we haven't forgotten the previous activist generation,
many of whom put the struggle ahead of a better life for themselves and
their children. We simply believe that this generation can make the commitment to the struggle *and* maintain individual pursuits.

tions, are familiar with their work. This is part of the problem with constructing a political movement in our generation. Their lack of recognition in part reflects Americans' contemporary national obsession with financial gain and the overall move away from social concerns.

I have not included creative artists with activist sensibilities nor professional athletes and other entertainers, including rap artists, who participate in activist work. For most of these types, their activism is part of their celebrity persona, or their activism is not their primary work, or they fail to seriously connect themselves to any community group or political organization. There is a strain of activism growing among hip-hop artists like Black Star, dead prez, the Coup, KRS-One, Lauryn Hill, and Wyclef Jean, but as activist-minded as their lyrics may be, as tuned in as they are to activists concerns, and as much as hip-hop generationers admire their politicized messages and activities, few are in the trenches day to day working to bring about change like those at the forefront of activism in our generation.

Also excluded from this list are the many intellectuals, including scholars, journalists, and attorneys, who limit their activism to their work. Given their growing ranks (again, a privilege afforded by the previous generation's struggles), such a list could easily number in the hundreds. Of course, none of this is to diminish their important work, which, more often than not, reinforces the legitimacy of activist concerns.

This group of activists reflects the range of activism going on in our generation and some of the unique models carrying it out. The list highlights young Black activists who have demonstrated that they are in this for the long haul, not just engaged in a passing fling, and it is limited to fifteen due to space constraints. My intention is to highlight both locally and nationally recognized young activists who aren't reinventing the wheel but are effectively placing our generation's issues into historical and political context. They have shown innovation and resolve in attempting to bring about social change and in the process reveal distinguishing characteristics of our generation.

THE ACTIVISTS

Ras Baraka, community organizer, Newark, New Jersey. That Ras is the son of famed poet-activist Amiri Baraka is not to be altogether dismissed. The two share some of the same political ideas, and clearly Ras has been shaped by his father's activism. But Ras continues to demonstrate that he is neither a clone of nor a mouthpiece for his father.

As a student at Howard University in the late 1980s, Baraka was president of the student body and fought to keep Lee Atwater from sitting on the Howard University board of trustees. As a student activist, Ras was also a co-founder of Black Nia F.O.R.C.E. (Freedom Organization for Racial and Cultural Enlightenment). Ras' strength has been his commitment and his consistency. He's demonstrated a commitment to youth as an eighth-grade teacher for the past nine years and a commitment to Newark, New Jersey, his hometown, where he continues to challenge political insiders to include the entire community, not just the wealthy. The focus of his activism reveals that he clearly understands the power of local politics. Equally important, he represents a symbolic link between the Black power generation and the hip-hop generation. This link is critical to Black baby boomers because it reminds them that all of their sacrifices were not in vain; there are hip-hop generationers who not only have learned important lessons from the previous generation's struggle but are also building on them. Although Ras Baraka has yet to succeed in becoming an elected official—he lost a race for mayor in 1994 and another for city councilman-at-large in 1998—time is on his side.

Thabiti Bruce Boone, co-founder and director of FIST (Fighting Ignorance, Spreading Truth), Rochester, New York. As a student activist at Rochester Institute of Technology in the mid- to late 1980s, Thabiti Boone set his sights on developing youth activists—beginning with his college peers and reaching out to Rochester-area high school students. Over the past fifteen years, he has not strayed from that mission. As a college student, Boone co-founded FIST, a student empowerment and youth activist organization in 1990. Since then his activism has centered on empowering youth through FIST's awareness programs, workshops, and forums for high school and college students. FIST annually reaches thousands of young people through its combined services, including lectures and citywide activities like its Yes to Success basketball camp and Kwanzaa program. In addition to community service, academic tutoring, and recreational programs, FIST goes beyond the run-of-the-mill youth program in that young people run the program from top to bottom. They make up the board of directors, the committees, and staffing—what Boone calls "youth empowered by youth." "Our goal has been to develop a new generation of community activists and leaders," says Boone. "There are tons of youth programs across the country, but few are tapping into the youth energy that has historically—before integration—been at the heart of the Black community." A single father for the past fifteen years, Boone is also active in the national fatherhood movement, advocating for fathers' rights and responsibilities. He is currently working to incorporate these efforts into FIST. "Whenever the Black family is talked about, no one talks about the father. But fatherhood is the new frontier as we look at the problems facing us as a community and as a family."

Jamal-Harrison Bryant, founder and pastor of the Empowerment Temple AME Church, Baltimore, Maryland. Spiritually centered activists like Jamal-Harrison Bryant dispel the myth that the Black church is out of touch with the problems facing this generation. Bryant is part of a generation of young ministers who are building on the activist-minded tradition of churches like Jaramogi Agyeman's Shrine of the Black Madonna, Jeremiah Wright's Trinity Church of Christ in Chicago, Reverend Frank Reid's AME Bethel Church in Baltimore, and others. Currently, Bryant is in the developmental stages of forming the Empowerment Temple, a church centered around community activism. "With the Empowerment Temple we are trying to build a paradigm as to what a social-activist church ought to look like." Formerly an assistant of Reverend Frank Reid at Baltimore's AME Bethel Church, Wright participated in Men of Bethel, a group of young men who organized community patrols that resulted in drastic reductions of crime in the area. Like many hip-hop generationers, Bryant was politicized by the Rodney King decision and subsequent riots. As a student at Morehouse College at the time, he put together the African American Student Alliance to conduct protests and demonstrations of outrage in Atlanta. As Director for the Youth and College Division of the NAACP from 1996 to 2000, Wright lobbied on Capitol Hill for youth-related issues, initiated the Stop the Violence Start the Love campaign in the wake of the killing of Notorious B.I.G., and was one of the coordinators for the Million Youth Movement. Wright also spearheaded the NAACP's protest of Webster's Dictionary's definition of "nigger" and protested the inequity in the selection of Supreme Court justice law clerks.

Wright plans to go beyond his efforts at the NAACP with his Empowerment Temple and indicates that he is not alone: "Young ministers like 30-year-old Ivan Douglass

Hicks in Indianapolis and 26-year-old Charles Jenkins in Chicago represent a whole generation of young ministers with a social mission that's on the rise." Wright says the Black church has taken a backseat to social institutions that came into existence as a result of the civil rights movement, but as programs like welfare and affirmative action give way, the church will resume its mission. Wright's Empowerment Temple requires church members to join the NAACP, register to vote, and read a book a month, in addition to participating in a host of cultural and political activities. "In this millennium," says Wright, "the church will have to go back to its original focus—to be all things to all people."

DeLacy Davis, founder and president of Black Cops Against Police Brutality (B-CAP), East Orange, New Jersey. A policeman in the East Orange Police Department (EOPD) since 1986, Sergeant DeLacy Davis founded the community-based group Black Cops Against Police Brutality in 1991. DeLacy credits a combination of events as his motivation: the birth of his daughter, dissatisfaction with what he had personally observed in law enforcement, and a speech by former Black Panther, and then recently freed political prisoner, Dhoruba Bin Wahad. "Dhoruba described how he was falsely imprisoned, and his comments hit home when he said, 'I know there are Black police officers in the room. If you punks won't stand up and defend your community, at least give us the information we need to defend ourselves.'" With chapters in Baltimore, St. Louis, Newark, and East Orange, the organization's mission is to improve community police relations, to be the conscience of the criminal justice system, and to enhance the quality of life for "people of African descent." B-CAP conducts workshops around the country for activist groups and individuals at churches, malls, community centers, schools, and even street corners.

The workshops cater especially to youth and involve role-playing scenarios, including what to do if you're stopped by the police, what to do if you're searched by the police, and what to do if you witness an incident of police brutality. Risking harm to themselves and their livelihoods, B-CAP members engage in protests against police brutality, speak out against brutal departments, and testify in court against abusive officers.

Another of the organization's notable feats is its commitment to turning over lawbreakers who want to turn themselves in but fear they will be beaten or killed by the police. "We make all the arrangements to turn them in, but also install safeguards to keep cops from beating confessions out of them, such as videotaping them to show what physical condition they were in when turned over," says Sergeant Davis. "We are advocates for the voiceless and take seriously the instant credibility that being a member of law enforcement gives us."

Donna Frisby-Greenwood, executive director for Philadelphia Inner City Games, co-chair for the Coalition of Black Youth Voters. Donna Frisby-Greenwood's focus on galvanizing the youth vote, her track record as a fund-raiser, and the familiarity she enjoys within public policy and activist circles distinguishes her among hip-hop generation activists. Frisby-Greenwood touched the lives of many hip-hop generationers through her work as development director and later co-executive director of Rock the Vote. During her tenure at Rock the Vote (1995–1998), she established the Hip-Hop Coalition for Political Power, a campaign that featured artists like Chuck D, LL Cool J, Method Man, and Snoop in public service announcements directed at African American and Latino youth. "As an activist in Philly, I had been working with hip-hop artists like Chuck D and Will Smith to reach young people. I knew it worked and had relevance." The effort registered around 70,000 18–24-year-old Blacks and Latinos. But Frisby's activism began long before Rock the Vote. In 1989, she co-founded Children First, a Philadelphia-based youth organization whose primary goal was to identify potential leaders (thirteen and fourteen-year-olds) and take them through a leadership development program. They arranged tutors to help the teens with their schoolwork, helped those whose families who were homeless find homes, helped those who had family members addicted to drugs get help, and helped illegal immigrants get citizenship. "In trying to teach them about the political process and help their families, I got involved politically, made sure their parents were registered to vote, and got the young people involved in political activities so they would register to vote when they came of age," Frisby-Greenwood recalls. "We also took the young people to the state capital to lobby for youth issues." Since then she's been committed to getting more young Blacks and Latinos involved in the political process. Her current involvement in local and national organizations, such as Inner City Games (which conducts computer and sports camps and after-school programs for young people living in low-income areas), REACH or Rappers Educating All Curricula through Hip-Hop (an organization she's helping Chuck D to develop that will use hip-hop as a teaching tool in the classroom), and the Coalition of Black Youth Voters (which works to get young people involved in local politics), continues to build on her already significant circle of influence and relevance to our generation.

Jesse Jackson Jr., Illinois congressman. Now in his third term in Congress, Jesse Jackson Jr. represents the 2nd District of Illinois, an area that includes Chicago's South Side and southern suburbs. Prior to being elected in 1996, he served as field director for the National Rainbow Coalition, which is where his career began. Jesse Jr. holds the distinction of sharing the first and last name of the Reverend Jesse Jackson, who had two high-profile presidential campaigns, but never held political office. The Reverend Jesse Jackson, though not an elected official, is a Washington insider in many respects. Routinely, he delivers votes and legitimacy to Democrats. That access, along with his long-term commitment to issues that matter to African Americans, has earned the Reverend Jesse Jackson the unofficial status of African American royalty in the same sense that the Kennedy family name endears its bearer to the general American public. That distinction has been passed down to Jesse Jr. Unlike Conrad Muhammad, who's earned his national recognition the hard way, Jesse Jr. gained it instantly due to the family name. Conrad has more grassroots appeal and hip-hop nation acceptance. Jesse Jr.'s appeal is mostly with Black middle-class hip-hop generationers, their parents, and their white peers. Jesse Jr.'s willingness to dabble in give-and-take exchanges with Republicans, such as his politicking for a south suburban Chicago airport, aligns him with new Black politicians who are more focused on getting results than simply being identified with the Democratic Party. This is not to take away from his liberal agenda, as he is often a spokesman on matters of race and poverty in the House. Like other hip-hop generation activists whose parents were civil rights/Black power leaders, Jesse Jr. represents the symbolic link between yesterday's and today's Black struggle. Serving a district that is 35 percent white and one-third suburban, Jesse Jr. has placed great emphasis on his cross-cultural appeal and on the new Black middle class. He has yet to reach out to hip-hop generationers in a way that distinguishes him as "our generation's leader." But as one who's come of age in our generation, he's not too far removed—despite his privileged upbringing—from the issues that matter to most hip-hop generationers.

Tamara Jones, community organizer, New York City, New Haven, Houston. Activists like Tamara Jones are much harder to pin down because they aren't always connected to one specific organization or cause. Jones' activism has included issues as diverse as police brutality, sexism, and capitalist exploitation, labor rights, and gay, lesbian, and transgender rights. She has helped to establish new organizations as well as worked within the structures of existing ones. "My own activist identity started out race-based, then incorporated gender, class, cross-gender, transsexual, etc.," explains Jones. "More and more, over the years I find my activism focused on trying to create a space where all of these things are present and talking to each other." As a member of the New York City–based Audre Lorde Project: Center for Lesbian, Gay, Bisexual, Two-Spirit & Transgender People of Color Communities, she helped develop the organization's Working Group Against Police Violence. The Working Group Against Police Violence helped to form the Coalition Against Police Brutality, a broader multirace and multigender coalition representing various organizations that had previously been demonstrating individually against police brutality in New York City. Since 1998 the coalition has held annual marches against police brutality and homophobia. "Because of the glaring gaps in the movement around police brutality we developed analysis that would reflect our experiences as Blacks as well as women, lesbian, gay, transgender, Latino, Asian, etc." Prior to working with the coalition, Jones co-founded Caribbean Pride, the only Caribbean gay and lesbian rights group in the United States, and participated in the formation of Black AIDS Mobilization (BAM), which conducted

AIDS awareness campaigns in African American and Caribbean American communities in New York City as early as 1992. Whether organizing around police brutality, AIDS awareness, or labor and union issues (as she did when helping to organize graduate student teaching assistants at Yale in the mid-1990s), she measures success by the degree to which the activism broadens the group's analysis. "What is important and exciting about our generation's activism," Jones emphasizes, "is that many of us in a post–civil rights era realize the limits of a race-only politics and realize that we can't talk about Black liberation without race, class, gender, sexual identity, or immigrant issues."

Van Jones, founder and national executive director of the Ella Baker Center for Human Rights, San Francisco. As an activist, Van Jones has focused much of his attention and legal expertise toward ending police abuse. His Ella Baker Center, founded in 1996, documents, exposes, and challenges human rights violations committed by law enforcement officers. The center grew out of an effort that began in 1994 called Bay Area Policewatch. Bay Area Policewatch maintains a hot line for victims of police misconduct in the Bay Area. Jones later duplicated this effort with New York Policewatch, which provides the same service for victims of police misconduct in New York City. Jones has been part of a growing local and national movement to end police brutality, harassment, profiling, and intimidation and has quickly gained the national attention of hip-hop generationers, for whom police brutality and high incarceration rates have been catalysts for activism. Beyond targeting police brutality, Jones has used his Ella Baker Center to help launch INS-Watch (a community group focused on ending immigration cop harassment), protest inhumane jail conditions, turn media attention on specific incidents of police abuse, as well as bring youth activism to bear on political issues specifically affecting youth such as California Proposition 21, which the enactment of Proposition 21 makes it easier for prosecutors to try kids as adults, limits juvenile probation, mandates one-year prison sentences for graffiti writing, and deems gang recruitment by middle school students a felony. Jones often joins forces with California-based youth activist groups like Youth Organizing Communities and Critical Resistance Youth Force. Jones' Ella Baker Center also helped develop the Third Eye Movement, a youth activist training and education organization that uses hip-hop music and video cameras to challenge police abuse.

Tonya McClary, community organizer and consultant with the National Coalition to Abolish the Death Penalty, Washington, D.C. McClary began honing her focus on criminal justice issues specifically affecting hip-hop generationers through her work as a fellow at Amnesty International, as an attorney in Baltimore's Office of the Public Defender, and as the director of research in the Criminal Justice Project for the NAACP Legal Defense and Educational Fund (LDEF). In 1998, while at LDEF she was involved in mobilizing public interest around the now infamous case of Kemba Smith, a young college student who received a mandatory minimum sentence for a drug conspiracy conviction after refusing to testify against her drug dealer boyfriend. The effort significantly raised public awareness on issues involving drug cases, conspiracy charges, and mandatory minimum sentencing. In 1999, she continued her commitment to "legal work that has an impact on the community" by joining on as co-counsel along with Malik Zulu Shabazz in defense of Patrice Peterson. Peterson was accused of sparking violence at the Million Youth March and was charged with two counts of assault and reckless endangerment. The trial ended with a hung jury.

Over the past few years her primary concern has been to develop a how-to manual for activists and attorneys to work together on death penalty cases. The basis for this model is her involvement in grassroots public education campaigns on various cases involving juveniles and the death penalty, including the high-profile capital punishment of Shaka Sankofa, formerly Gary Graham, who was executed in Huntsville, Texas, in June 2000. Sankofa had been sentenced to death for a 1981 murder committed when he was seventeen. In 1997, McClary was involved in strumming up community support for Azi Kambule, a seventeen-year-old South African charged with capital murder in Mississippi. The case gained national attention, and Kambule was spared the death penalty. Currently, McClary is bringing this same model of activism to bear on other cases involving the death penalty, such as Chicago's Deathrow 10. As for the future direction of her activism: "Whatever I'm involved in," she says, "is going to be about trying to put criminal justice into the broader civil rights and human rights frameworks."

Conrad Muhammad, founder and director of A Movement for Conscious Hip-Hop Activism Necessary for Global Empowerment (CHHANGE), New York City. One of the most nationally recognizable activists in the hip-hop generation, Conrad Muhammad entered our generation's collective consciousness and made his presence felt as an activist as a young, outspoken member of the Nation of Islam (NOI) in the early 1980s. As a undergraduate student at the University of Pennsylvania, Conrad became National Youth Minister for the Nation of Islam in 1988 and remained a minister in the nation for nearly a decade. During much of this time, he helped Nation of Islam leaders to tap into and channel the rebelliousness and popularity of the hip-hop community, something that other Black activist and/or religious groups have yet to duplicate with any measure of success. The Nation of Islam along with Khallid Muhammad and Conrad Muhammad were largely responsible for politicizing many hip-hop generationers in some shape, form, or fashion. By 1991, Conrad was named minister of Harlem's infamous Nation of Islam Mosque #7, a post that afforded him even greater visibility and prestige. Conrad's image as young, unapologetically Black, outspoken, and widely visible in an organization that in the minds of youth belonged to the previous generation made the Nation of Islam attractive to a whole new generation and simultaneously fueled concern for Black activist issues among a wider range of hip-hop generationers. The pro-Black rhetoric of rap groups like Public Enemy, X-Clan, Poor Righteous Teachers, Ice Cube, and others were inspired by this loose association between the Nation of Islam and the hip-hop community. The growing ranks of young Blacks in America's prison system and the NOI presence there as well only strengthened this connection. Many hip-hop generationers saw Conrad Muhammad as the heir-apparent of Louis Farrakhan and the obvious leader of the NOI for our time. His abrupt departure from the Nation of Islam in 1998, after more than a decade in the organization, left many of us wondering who would assume the next generation of leadership of one of Black America's most significant religious groups. Currently, he's attempting to channel the popularity he enjoys with hip-hop generationers into a new organization that hints toward a future for him in electoral politics. He is well loved and admired among hip-hop generationers, and his future as an activist and leader among hip-hop generationers is secure.

Shannon Reeves, president of Oakland chapter of the NAACP, Oakland, California. Like many hip-hop generationers, Shannon Reeves can't be pigeonholed. He gives a whole new meaning to concepts like Republican, liberal, and Black. The image of an NAACP leader who, on the one hand, leads a lawsuit against UPS for discriminating against Black drivers and, on the other hand, celebrates George W. Bush's GOP nomination on national television is hard for many to swallow. When he took the helm as president of the Oakland chapter of the NAACP in 1996, more than a few eyebrows raised at the mention of his political party affiliation. His brash style and attacks on the old guard Black leadership gave him instant national recognition. He has created a bigger wave than most ever imagined and not just because he's both a Republican and an NAACP member. By the end of his second term in 2000, the chapter was in better shape financially than it had been in years. Mostly it is his innovative, youth-centered approach to politics that distinguishes Reeves as a hip-hop generation activist. He has transformed the chapter from an organization of primarily baby boomers to one that includes younger members. In the process, he has increased membership from 900 to 4,000 and has made self-help and economic development central to the chapter's work. But Reeves is no newcomer. He is an Oakland native and has been active in the NAACP since his early teens. At seventeen, he was elected to the organization's national board. He has also held ten other positions in the NAACP, including youth leader and regional director. And his efforts goes beyond the NAACP. Reeves also heads his own non-profit economic development organization, the Freedom Fund. Reeves holds lasting value to hip-hop generationers in that he's pushed the envelope on political identity: not only is he a Republican (that's easy), but he's a Black Republican who continues to identify with issues important to the Black community, a Republican whose support base is Black, and a Republican who continues to work for change in the Black community. Given that he expressed political interest with an unsuccessful run for mayor of Oakland in 1998 and the popularity he enjoys with young Republicans, Democrats, and Independents alike, it's clear that Reeves is among those who will help to broaden the scope of the mainstream political process.

Malik Zulu Shabazz, national coordinator and legal counsel for the Million Youth March, Washington, D.C. While an undergraduate at Howard University, Malik Zulu Shabazz founded a student activist group called Unity Nation. Shabazz came to national recognition as a law student at Howard who led on-campus rallies in defense of Khallid Muhammad's right to speak at the university in 1994. Prior to the Howard controversy, Muhammad had been suspended as national spokesman for the Nation of Islam by Minister Louis Farrakhan, Muhammad's 1993 speech at Kean College had been condemned by Congress, and some national Black leaders had publicly denounced him. In June 1998, armed with assault rifles, Shabazz, Muhammad, and members of the New Black Panthers held a demonstration in Jasper, Texas, to counter a Ku Klux Klan march in the wake of the lynching of James Byrd.

Around that time, Shabazz, again with Muhammad, was one of the primary organizers who put out the call for the Million Youth March, which took place in Harlem the following September. Shabazz's input helped to keep the march's goals on the pulse of the hip-hop generation; he advocated independent security patrols in Black communities, reparations from the American government for the descendants of enslaved Africans, and uniting the nation's Black youth (including gang members) to bring about positive social change, among other things. And it was the savvy legal maneuverings of Shabazz's legal team that helped secure permits for the march, in spite of Mayor Rudy Giuliani's efforts to change its location or cancel it. This feat alone was a major victory for hip-hop generationers, for whom Giuliani has come to personify today's war on youth. But Giuliani wasn't the march's only opponent. A countermarch, dubbed the Million Youth Movement, held in Atlanta on the same weekend by old-guard Black organizations like Operation PUSH, the NAACP, and the Nation of Islam revealed a division in Black leadership. The Khallid Muhammad/Malik Zulu Shabazz school called for youth to take the lead, whereas the old guard seemed to guide the march in Atlanta. In his comments about the march, Shabazz repeatedly referred to himself and other hip-hop generationers as a "new Black leadership"—one that isn't "chosen by white America." It is an old slogan steeped in NOI rhetoric, but one that rings true with the hip-hop generation, and it explains why young Blacks continue to find Shabazz palatable, despite his Jew bashing. Following the untimely death of Khallid Muhammad in 2001, Shabazz became national chairman of the New Black Panthers. Given the moderate success of the Million Youth March, Shabazz's interest in seeking political office, his ability to speak to the alienation of Black youth, and his consistency in placing that frustration at the forefront of his political agenda make him particularly attractive to hip-hop generationers.

Lateefah Simon, executive director, Center for Young Women's Development, San Francisco. Incarceration rates for young women, which have climbed to an all-time high in our lifetime, is a critical issue for hip-hop generation activists like Lateefah Simon. Simon came to work at the Center for Young Women's Development (CYWD) as a community outreach worker at the age of seventeen. At the time, the organization focused its efforts on educating young women of color on health issues and safety, as well as providing job referrals to unemployed young women and shelter to the homeless.

Realizing that the organization needed to reach young women where they were, Simon pushed the organization to go beyond its initial mission in order to disrupt the cycle of poverty and reduce the recidivism rates of young women in the juvenile justice system. Her enthusiasm led her to take on the role of executive director at the age of twenty. Under Simon's leadership, the CYWD evolved into an organization that conducts workshops for young women at San Francisco's Juvenile Hall and at local crack houses. The sessions are designed to provide young women economic self-sufficiency and the tools needed to navigate the criminal justice system. The programs are staffed entirely by former juvenile offenders, all women under the age of twenty-five. "Visiting prisons it became clear to me that something was wrong with the system, given the majority of people of color contained there," says Simon describing the evolution of her activist work. "The focus of my activism is to bring other young people into activism around these and related issues."

To that end, Simon uses the CYWD and its programs as a springboard to delve into other issues. She was one of the primary organizers of the 1998 Schools Not Jails student walk-out, a demonstration that involved approximately 5,000 Bay Area students. She has organized young people around the issues of domestic violence and HIV/AIDS and has worked with the Pro-Choice Education Project and the Treatment on Demand Council to ensure that young people have access to detox services. She was also involved in organizing youth opposition to Proposition 21. "CYWD serves as a stepping stone for young men and women who haven't thought about these issues," Simon explains. "We use the Black Panthers Save the People philosophy—meet people's basic needs first and then let them know there is a larger movement that young people not only need to get involved in, but need to get in at the frontline."

Lisa Sullivan, founder and president of Local Initiative,
Support, Training, and Education Network, Incorporated
(LISTEN, Inc.), Washington, D.C.   A youth organizer and
activist throughout much of the 1980s and 1990s, Sullivan
gained national recognition as the director of the field division of the Children's Defense Fund. While at the Children's
Defense Fund, she helped create and direct the Black Student Leadership network. She took her interest in training
activists to the next logical level by founding LISTEN, Inc.,
in 1998. "We see ourselves as institutionalizing the role that
Ella Baker played for the Student Non-Violent Coordinating
Committee (SNCC)," Sullivan says. "Baker helped create a
space for young activists, but many of her protégés didn't do
the same for our generation."

The D.C.-based LISTEN sees the involvement of urban
youth as critical to any meaningful program of action dealing with the problems caused by urban neglect, poverty, police brutality, and high incarceration rates of hip-hop generationers. Targeting youth ages 14–29 years old, LISTEN
approaches these problems in three main ways. (1) At the
national level, they work with executive directors and/or
presidents of existing mainstream organizations whose programs aren't reaching as many young people as they should.
LISTEN bridges the gap by advocating that the true leadership for these organizations, if they are to be effective, lies in
the community's natural youth leaders. (2) LISTEN trains
the existing staff of these institutions to work with youth,
and trains young people in leadership skills. (3) In some
communities where the existing institutions aren't willing to
meet youth halfway, LISTEN works with young people
to build their own organizations.

What distinguishes Sullivan's approach is her insis-
tence that youth must assume the mantle of leadership and
LISTEN's commitment to identifying and nurturing this

leadership. Sullivan says this leadership is not always found in expected places; it may be the young woman who braids everyone's hair, the daycare worker, those in the nightclubs that everyone connects with. "These are the natural leaders," Sullivan says. "During the '80s and '90s, the public sector turned young Black folk into the problem. In the middle of this war on youth, we created a world that enabled us to survive that is beneath the radar screen of mainstream society. That is the leadership that needs to be identified." When talking about LISTEN's agenda, Sullivan sometimes sounds like she's training entrepreneurs. She explains: "This is a direct response to our generation's sense that many of the older generation's organizations are dysfunctional and haven't produced a new leadership because many of the people running them don't have basic organizational skills. Our people deserve accountable organizations that run effectively."

Baye Wilson, community organizer, Newark, New Jersey. Wilson is representative of a stream of activists in the hip-hop generation who intertwine their professional lives with their activist ones. Wilson says that because there are so many hip-hop generationers from all walks of life engaging in activism, this generation has escaped the notion of "the" Black leader. "No one has risen to the popularity of a Malcolm or Martin," he says. Noting that with so many leaders, current movements can't be disrupted by stopping individuals. Wilson currently co-chairs the National Conference of Black Lawyers. Additionally, he has worked on campaigns to free Black political prisoners, including Mumia Abu-Jamal and Sundiata Acoli. He has also worked on the Hands Off Assata Campaign, which aims to stop the U.S. government from extraditing Assata Shakur. As an entertainment lawyer, he bridges his legal work and activist work, providing legal representation for rap artists like dead prez, the Coup, and Headrush. "I made a conscious effort to work with politically conscious rap artists. In addition to providing them with protection in a ruthless industry, it sets up a parameter for us to build together on other issues." Such issues include his role as an organizer and board member of the Black August Collective, an organization that promotes hip-hop concerts in Cuba and New York. "In 1995 a group of us got together to try to build a movement around educating the younger generation on the significance of Cuba. Given the influence of hip-hop and the growth of hip-hop in Cuba, we thought this was the best way to raise awareness around the issue of political prisoners, exiles, police brutality, and the prison industrial complex." Artists like Common, dead prez, and Black Star have participated in past years. The proceeds from the concerts go to families of Black political prisoners and toward building a studio for rap artists in Cuba. As a full-time attorney working on neighborhood planning and development, Wilson doesn't let his day job get in the way of his activism. As director of the New Jersey office of Regional Plan Association, he's currently developing an arts and cultural district in Newark. "I'm working with community-based organizations so that residents can shape their lives in a way that is reflective of their true needs. I'm trying to bring a radical analysis to everything I do—whether it's urban planning, entertainment law, or organizing."

Too often voices like these are missing from efforts to create the institutional structure needed to move the hip-hop generation into political power. With these vibrant strains of activism in the hip-hop generation in mind, we can more carefully consider the political agenda for the hip-hop generation.

7

THE POLITICS OF THE HIP-HOP GENERATION

Identifying a Political Agenda

PROMINENT BLACKS AND WHITES GIVIN' ORDERS FOR
  MASS SLAUGHTERS
I WANT ALL MY DAUGHTERS TO BE LIKE MAXINE
  WATERS
              —KRS-ONE, "CIA (CRIMINALS IN ACTION)"

DURING THE 2000 PRESIDENTIAL CAMPAIGN, RAP MUSIC mogul Russell Simmons announced that he was turning his attention to how best to bring the hip-hop generation into the mainstream political process. "With issues like racial profiling and police brutality taking a center stage in this year's elections, the hip-hop community needs to mobilize, move as an army, and make their voice heard," said Simmons, joined by Al Sharpton, Martin Luther King III, Conrad Muhammad, and others at a press conference in a Manhattan hotel. Simmons' effort, dubbed Rap the Vote 2000, joined forces with Rock the Vote, a ten-year-old organization that focuses on getting 18–24-year-old music fans involved in civic activism and registered to vote. Together they hoped to register thousands of American youths. With the catchy, hip-hop-inspired slogan "Register. Vote. Represent.," Simmons planned to use his Web site 360Hip-hop.com, public service announcements, and joint political forums and fundraising events with Rock the Vote as a means of "educating and empowering" hip-hop generationers.

Although Simmons effort has been the most high-profile attempt from within the hip-hop community to get hip-hop generationers tuned in to the political process, it wasn't the first. Rap the Vote 2000, in fact, was an attempt to relaunch Rap the Vote, an earlier move by Rock the Vote to register young Black and Latino voters. And efforts at turning young Blacks' attention to public policy and the mainstream political process have taken other forms. Since the mid-1990s, the rap music magazine *The Source* has reported on youth sociopolitical issues directly linked to hip-hop's cultural movement. Similar efforts to inform and politicize the hip-hop generation have come out of competing rap magazines like *Rap Pages*, *XXL*, and *Vibe*. Radio personality Davey D has taken this style of reporting to a new level with his on-line FNV (Friday Night Vibe) newsletter, which offers weekly commentary and news about rap figures, hip-hop activists, and youth political issues. He has been sending out his weekly dispatches since 1996, keeping hip-hop generationers informed on issues ranging from Proposition 21 to police brutality.

Rap artists like Lauryn Hill, The Goodie Mob, Common, the Coup, and others have made it their mission to help politicize this generation through their lyrics and public appearances. In the months leading up to the 2000 presidential election, rapper and talk show host Queen Latifah joined clothier Lane Bryant in a nationwide print campaign aimed at registering 60 million young people, telling them to "click and be heard" by registering on-line at Election.com. Former Nation of Islam minister Conrad Muhammad, with his A Movement for Conscious Hip-Hop Activism Necessary for Global Empowerment (CHHANGE), is in the early stages of also trying to access this virtually untapped voter pool. In addition to getting youth involved in protests and demonstrations, the organization is attempting to register 1 million young voters. CHHANGE is also challenging rappers to run for political office and get involved in politics at the local level.

These efforts often point to voter apathy among young Black and Latino voters, echoing Black and white mainstream leaders. It is peculiar that voter apathy is such a considerable problem in a country that espouses internationally the value of civic participation and among a racial group whose parents were instrumental in making the idea of America inextricably bound to voting rights. However, hip-hop generationers have come of age at the time of an emerging global economy, which has negatively affected income for most working-class Americans; many young people are focused on careers as a means of securing individual and family economic well-being. At the same time, many young Blacks see the global economy and the many social problems resulting from it—high unemployment, which leads to the underground economy, gangs, and high rates of prison incarceration—as a failure of the political system. In their view, policy makers—in their termination of welfare programs, in their passing of mandatory minimum sentencing laws, in their weakening of affirmative action, in their failure to ensure for Black children an equal education—have worked against young Blacks, not for them. Furthermore, many conclude that if the political mainstream has not worked for the civil rights/Black power generation—which did manage to achieve some social gains—how can it possibly work for us, a generation that can point to no substantial gains but only losses? Does voter apathy mean that we are without a political agenda? And if not, what exactly is the political agenda of young Blacks in their twenties and thirties?

A POLITICAL AGENDA

Although it has yet to be articulated as such, hip-hop generationers do have a concrete political agenda. Snippets of this agenda often gain expression in individual commentary, such as that coming from Russell Simmons, Conrad Muhammad, Davey D, and others, rap lyrics from more politically minded rappers like Lauryn Hill, the Goodie Mob, and the Coup, activists such as Oakland NAACP head Shannon Reeves, hip-hop journalists like Akiba Solomon and Ta-Nehisi Coates, and even sporadically from some old-guard Black activists (like Jesse Jackson) and politicians (like Maxine Waters). Although this agenda has yet to be articulated holistically, it centers around seven main issues: education, employment and workers rights, reparations, economic infrastructure in urban communities, youth poverty and disease, anti-youth legislation, and foreign policy. These issues resonate with hip-hop generationers for reasons that are tied to the social and political landscape.

1. Education.   In today's economy, it is increasingly difficult to secure jobs that pay a living wage without higher education. Public schools throughout the nation's center cities are not equipped with the personnel and resources to produce students who can compete with their more well-to-do peers. As many hip-hop generationers struggle to make a living in today's world, they support any changes at the elementary and secondary levels (public and private) that will prepare young Blacks for employment options in a high-tech, global economy. Hip-hop generationers welcome the elimination of disparities in educational attainment rates (at the high school, college, and postgraduate levels), including disparities in access to competent teachers and administrators, books, computers, adequate facilities and programs, the Internet, and internships. The rising costs of a college education continue to make college unattainable for many American youth. Hip-hop generationers would support government control of the exorbitant and growing cost of an education and the creation of financial aid policies that can meet contemporary challenges.

2. Employment and Workers' Rights. The hip-hop generation, more than any other demographic, can attest to the economic crisis faced by American workers as high-paying manufacturing jobs exit the country in search of cheaper labor. Hip-Hop generationers would support economic policies that would encourage the retention and creation of jobs for working-class Americans that allowed them to afford homes, cars, vacations, health care, and safe and effective child care. Along with these changes, hip-hop generationers would welcome policies that would end racial disparities in employment rates, rates of pay, and home financing loans.

3. Reparations. The issue of reparations has galvanized serious national political interest among African Americans in the past few years. Although Black power grassroots activist organizations (such as N'COBRA, the Republic of New Africa, and the Nation of Islam) have pressed for reparations since the 1960s and 1970s, the hip-hop generation put the issue on the map of youth concerns in 1998 with the Million Youth March. (Reparations was one of the

March's demands.) Most hip-hop generationers do not expect reparations in the form of a cash payment or a partition of land that would essentially constitute a separate country within a country—things once advocated by some civil rights/Black power generationers. For us, it's fundamentally a question of respect. Centuries of unpaid labor can be repaid in more creative ways. Young Black voters would support reparations goals that don't stigmatize Blacks and don't take the form of hand-outs. Hip-hop generationers would probably support any reparations policy that included the following: honoring the descendants of enslaved Africans and Black veterans; setting the historical record straight on slavery, teaching it in our schools, and commemorating it on our holidays; erecting monuments and museums that celebrate Black contributions to America. Goals like these would demonstrate that the country is committed to upholding its creed of self-evident truths.

4. Economic Infrastructure in Urban Communities. Black communities like the South Side and West Side of Chicago, North Side of Philadelphia, Harlem and other parts of New York City, and South Central Los Angeles have the appearance of cities recently at war: dilapidated housing, gutted buildings, pothole-filled streets, and little economic activity. The love hip-hop generationers have for their home cities is evident by the race by kids across the country to put their city on the hip-hop map. Economic revitalization efforts like those advocated by Congressman Charles Rangel in Harlem are a good start. It's no accident that when some hip-hop generation entertainers and athletes (such as Tyrese and Black Starr) who rise from poverty to notoriety and want to give back in a big way attempt to build businesses or community centers in the 'hood. Any attempt to rebuild the economic infrastructure of urban America would resonate with hip-hop generationers and would receive support from young Black voters.

5. *Youth Poverty and Disease.*   Young Blacks are not inherently prone to poverty or disease. Hip-hop generationers realize this and are waiting for legislators to catch up. This generation will support efforts to address public health concerns that disproportionately affect young Blacks like high rates of AIDS and HIV infection. Hip-hop generationers would support programs that encourage media outlets to be more responsible in reporting on these issues rather than showcasing statistics on racial gaps in these areas, which tend to imply Black inferiority.

6. *Anti-Youth Legislation.*   Hip-hop generationers support the re-evaluation of state and federal mandatory minimum sentencing laws passed in the 1980s and 1990s that have contributed to the enormous growth in the prison population, specifically the "three strikes" laws, the Continuing Criminal Enterprise Act, the Racketeering Influenced Corruption Organization Act, and laws governing co-conspirator testimony against petty drug dealers and people loosely associated with them. Because these high rates of imprisonment have disenfranchised a significant percentage of Black voters, hip-hop generationers support policies that would allow convicted felons who have served their time and paid their debt to society to resume their voting privileges—automatically, not through burdensome procedures.

A complete transformation in the style of policing in Black urban communities, particularly as it differs from suburban majority white communities, would receive support from young Black voters, as would a re-evaluation of policies that allow officers to operate above the law, especially as it relates to the ease with which murder can be deemed justifiable.

7. Foreign Policy. Like many voters, young Blacks would like to see their government enact a foreign policy agenda that at the very least isn't choking the life out of people of African descent (economically or environmentally) on the continent, in Caribbean island nations, and elsewhere. Hip-hop generationers believe that if indeed America has a healthy colorless policy at home, it ought to be reflected in its policy abroad as well.

Like all Americans, young Blacks want to be able to provide descent and safe housing, food, and education for themselves and their children. World conflicts and threats to national security that require U.S. military intervention usually hit close to home for hip-hop generationers, given the number of African Americans and Latinos in the military. Many hip-hop generationers, their relatives, or friends were on the ground in the Persian Gulf War and were involved in the peacekeeping missions in Bosnia and Somalia, and they are concerned about the lack of a similar commitment to restoring order and building an economic infrastructure in Black urban communities at home.

Black-on-Black gun violence and murder, which result from what is now an essential underground economy, are far more serious problems than police brutality. At the root are lack of employment options and inadequate economic infrastructure in urban communities. The domino effect of underground economy, police brutality, Black-on-Black violence, and prison incarceration could be seriously curtailed with descent-paying jobs, economic development, and a broad-sweeping plan to lift urban communities out of poverty. Hip-hop generationers support policies that bring urban communities into parity with suburban ones. Suburban life escapes the severity of these problems not by nature but by design. Urban communities deserve the same.

THE ESTABLISHMENT PROBLEM

These core concerns have not been integrated, in any substantial way, into any agenda within the mainstream political process—not into a political party platform, nor into the platforms of any of the traditional leading Black organizations. This is partly due to the old-guard Black leadership's unwillingness to take young Blacks seriously as a political force. This neglect has had three main outcomes. First, it has diminished the viability of the hip-hop generation's political agenda. Second, it has increased the feeling of futility among those in the hip-hop generation in even having a political agenda. And finally, this oversight has contributed to the failure of Black leadership to articulate any effective agenda beyond 1960s civil rights rhetoric, which has been universally co-opted by the Democratic, and even Republican, establishment.

Although the ideas at the core of the civil rights era are still relevant to today's political landscape (equality, inclusion, and the like), the manner in which they are now being articulated does not translate meaningfully into the ways these issues are manifest among the younger generation. In their attempt to fulfill their generation's own political goals, many Black baby boomers lost sight of the significance of the emerging generation.

By the mid-1960s and early 1970s, Blacks of all generations were beginning to get more involved in the mainstream political process, encouraged by the victories of civil rights legislation (such as the Civil Rights Act of 1964 and the Voting Rights Act of 1965), burgeoning Black culture, and awakening Black political power. The emergence of the Lowndes County Freedom Party in Alabama in 1965 and the national aftermath of Black voter participation following the Gary,

Indiana, Black Political Convention of 1972 revealed to many that the mainstream political process offered possibilities. In the 1970s, government jobs allowed many Blacks to attain a middle-class lifestyle, gave Blacks confidence in the country, and instilled civic pride. Between 1964 and 1984, Black voter participation steadily increased. As a result, during this time period we witnessed an increase in the number of Black elected officials for the first time since Reconstruction. The Jesse Jackson 1984 presidential campaign also brought many Blacks voters to the polls. However, Jackson's subsequent move away from the idea of forming a third party contributed to a general loss of hope for many formerly inspired by Jackson. In addition, the dismal economic prospects facing most young Blacks in the late 1980s and early 1990s led to a diminishment in the confidence in the political process. From 1984 to 1996, Black voter participation decreased from 54 to 46 percent.

For hip-hop generationers, it is difficult to find instances where Black baby boomers in mainstream leadership are collectively making a difference in the lives of young Blacks, who constitute a significant portion of Black America. Of course, there are cases where individual Black leaders, such as Maxine Waters, Jesse Jackson, and Al Sharpton, weigh in effectively on issues that affect the hip-hop generation. But Black politicians like Philadelphia Mayor John F. Street seem to be the norm on the political landscape. Street's moment to do the hip-hop generation proud came in the weeks leading up the 2000 Republican National Convention with the re-lease of a videotape showing Philadelphia police appre-hending and severely beating thirty-year-old Thomas Jones. At the time of the beating, Jones had already been shot five times. But rather than address police brutality, a critical issue for hip-hop generationers, Street shamelessly towed the party line. In a July 18, 2000, appearance on the Tavis Smiley

Show, Street, when pressed again and again by Smiley to give his honest opinion on the indisputably inhumane beating and abuse of power, never condemned the beating but kept reiterating that this was not a Rodney King incident, referring to the 1991 police beating that set off the Los Angeles race riots of 1992. Street also used the Rodney King reference to suggest that the beating had nothing to do with race, implying that if Jones had been white, Black and white officers would have taken the same course of action. This is the type of Black leadership that has turned young Blacks off to the political process. This brand of leadership (both Black and white) is so intent on not playing "the race card" (that is, upset their white constituency by drawing attention to America's racial problems) that they are willing to deny these problems and ask us to do the same.

Organizations like the NAACP are likewise often out of synch with the hip-hop generation. Even though NAACP head Kweisi Mfume has represented African Americans well as head of the Congressional Black Caucus, under his watch the NAACP has missed the mark with the issues that matter most to Black youth. Many hip-hop generationers were stunned, disappointed, or confused by the NAACP's decision to spearhead the Million Youth Movement around the same time as the Million Youth March. If organizing youth around issues that concerned them was such a good and important idea, why didn't the NAACP support the Million Youth March already in motion rather than putting out a call for a counter-march, forcing young Blacks to choose between the two? For more and more hip-hop generationers, the NAACP plays itself out as an organization without focus or engagement with youth. It seemed to be gaining momentum during Ben Chavis' lead as executive director in 1993–1994 where he placed much of his focus on working more closely with far too long marginalized Black nationalist activists and getting more hip-hop generationers involved. But with Chavis' dismissal in August 1994, these efforts all but disappeared. Today the NAACP's most high-profile issues, while symbolic and important, don't change policy or affect ideology. Oftentimes, as in the case of the Million Youth Movement, the organization seems more concerned with selecting its issues with one-upmanship in mind, the goal being to secure the coveted position of The Black Leader of the moment. Lesser campaigns like the one against *Webster's* definition of the word "nigger" and the battle against the state of South Carolina for continuing to fly the Confederate flag atop the statehouse, although important attacks on continued racism in America, pale in comparison with discrepancies facing Black youth in the workforce (from hiring to pay) and the need to develop economic infrastructure in Black urban communities—issues that the NAACP pays lip service to but doesn't tackle with the same vigor.

In as far as the issues at the heart of the hip-hop generation's political agenda have yet to resonate with civil rights Black leadership, they have most certainly not gained expression among traditional political party leaders. Political insiders lament Blacks like Minister Louis Farrakhan who continue to challenge clear-cut instances of American racism. To bring up the issue of racial inequality in this manner, they say, is divisive. But what of substance have Blacks secured from the mainstream political process in the past ten or even twenty years that would make us feel like a respected part of American society?

The Democratic Party, the Republican Party, and the mainstream political process in general have a long history of marginalizing African Americans. This tendency persists today and has grown even more severe in the wake of the Black mainstream leadership's inability to move beyond the rhetoric of civil rights. True to form, in the 2000 presidential campaign, race remained at best on the periphery. Neither candidate thought enough of race to include any pressing racial concerns as platform issues.

If issues like reparations, economic development, youth crime and punishment, education, employment and workers rights, and youth poverty and disease aren't addressed by Black political groups like the NAACP and Urban League, these organizations will continue to lack credibility, influence, and appeal with America's Black youth. If they aren't addressed by mainstream political parties, Black voter participation will continue to decline. Republicans tired of Black voter affinity for the Democratic Party need only include any of these issues on their platform and watch the Black vote slip the Democrats' choke hold. Democrats who lament the lack of young Black voter participation and claim they want to do the right thing need only include any of these issues on their platform and watch young Black voters pour in. Third-party contenders who want to break the mainstream process's mold of catering to the economic elite should consider how such issues would resonate on their political agenda in a country dogged by unresolved racial issues.

A SOUND VEHICLE?

Perhaps it is overly optimistic to expect old-guard Black leadership or traditional parties to realize that placing issues central to ignored voting blocs on the national agenda is critical to salvaging any future of wide participation in mainstream politics. It seems logical that a force from within hip-hop's cultural movement would be the most sound vehicle to bring the hip-hop generation's political interests into the mainstream political process. Although efforts mounted from within the hip-hop movement hold great promise, to date most have been steeped in political naiveté, partisan politics, or petty bourgeois radicalism.

Consider Rap the Vote 2000, led by Russell Simmons. Simmons and company pointed to police brutality and racial profiling as critical issues for mobilizing hip-hop generationers, but a *Daily News* editorial penned by Simmons in June 2000 called for more police officers of color in Black communities as a solution to police brutality. Such a proposal makes the faulty assumption that the problem is with the color of the officers' skin and not with policing itself. Hip-hop generationers who have faced police brutality and racial profiling know that countless Black officers have been as notoriously abusive as some of their white counterparts. Most hip-hop generationers, though not mobilized as voters, are politicized to the point that they are aware of this. Strategies such as creating independent civilian complaint review boards that have subpoena power and immediately interviewing police officers involved in shootings (just as any other suspects) would have been more effective starting points. Any vehicle purporting to speak for hip-hop generationers, or any other constituency for that matter, ought to have at the very minimum a firm understanding of that group's interests and be able to clearly articulate them, if they are going to lead voters to the polls in any meaningful way.

A second red flag came with the group's announcement that it intended to have an impact on the 2000 presidential race—five months before the election. In such a time frame, little could realistically be done other than very limited voter registration. Voter registration, for a voting bloc or interest group whose political agenda has yet to be articulated in the mainstream, has little effect without voter education.

The Simmons effort was further discredited because from the start it was clear that the group was intent on bringing

Black and Latino votes to the Democratic Party. At the press conference, Simmons was joined by notable Democrats. Furthermore, Simmons raised funds for Hillary Rodham Clinton's run for the Senate from the state of New York and repeatedly lashed out against her then opponent Republican Mayor Rudy Giuliani. Like Giuliani, Mrs. Clinton has yet to commit herself to any of the central issues on the hip-hop generation's political agenda. Why then should she receive Black and Latino youth votes? This is the type of amateurish politicking that has disenchanted hip-hop generationers with old-guard Black leadership. How long can such maneuvers, even with a hip-hop face, sustain the interest of hip-hop generationers?

Finally, any effort to secure political power for hip-hop generationers should be devoid of anyone's financial interests. When the city of New York denied Rap the Vote 2000 a permit for a rally in Manhattan, they pointed to the fact that among the sponsors were Simmons' own for-profit businesses. Whatever Giuliani's intent, this points to yet another red flag on the Simmons effort. The Rap the Vote 2000 kick-off was tied to the launching of Simmons' on-line venture 360Hip-hop.com. Though it may not have been the case, the entire Rap the Vote 2000 effort reeked of a marketing ploy.

Rap the Vote 2000 generated a great deal of excitement among hip-hop generation activists and politically minded youth in search of an organizational model that defines our issues and our time. Simmons' effort may be the best thing we've seen to date, but it is by no means the best we can expect.

It may be more effective to channel the energy and momentum of hip-hop generationers somewhere closer to the periphery rather than the core of the hip-hop establishment, where political thought seems to be less clouded by dollar signs. The evolution of the self-proclaimed hip-hop minister's thinking since leaving the Nation of Islam in 1998 shows that Conrad Muhammad is ahead of the curve as far as moving hip-hop generationers closer to actualizing political power. He's not a hip-hop industry insider and is not part of the clique of folks who have gotten wealthy as movers and shakers in hip-hop, so his intentions don't seem to be dictated by just another hip-hop hustle. Moreover, his longtime involvement in the Nation of Islam has helped shape his political perspective. He understands what is at stake, understands the sociopolitical history, has credibility, and is able to put the issues into a context that is relevant to hip-hop generationers.

His first power move after leaving the Nation was founding A Movement for CHHANGE, which to date hasn't gotten far beyond voter registration, demonstrations, forums, and marches to realize its larger vision. "Ultimately the organization we are building is a hip-hop version of Operation PUSH, or a present-day combination of SNCC and the Black Panther Party," says Muhammad. Beyond this, he has been effective in helping hip-hop generationers see how issues that seem irrelevant are affecting our lives. "We don't have colored-only water fountains or a Vietnam War, so we have to more carefully show young people how political issues are affecting them." Part of what has helped him get his message out has been his post–Nation of Islam career as a radio talk show host, again as the hip-hop minister. After hosting a program on WLIB for several years, Muhammad now hosts "Sunday Night Live with Minister Conrad Muhammad" on New York City's WBLS. He has also been a visible participant and sometime consultant for Russell Simmons' Rock the Vote 2000.

Muhammad admits that funding has been a problem for his Movement for CHHANGE. When that problem is solved, he may be well on his way to a creating the effective advocacy group that hip-hop generationers need. All of the above suggests that even if his organization proves not to be the definitive one, he is drumming up the type of support that should make him a key player when hip-hop generationers finally find a vehicle to bring our political agenda onto the national stage. "We will make the political establishment understand that this is a generation that has not only produced a culture that has seized the center stage of the world, but that in terms of politics will be the most savvy of any generation that Black America has produced," Muhammad says. "We intend to put them on notice that they will have to vie for this generation's vote and reward it with substance or they won't get it."

Clearly Muhammad's long-term vision goes beyond his own group and speaks to the larger political process as it affects African Americans of all ages. He continues: "Politics is not the only solution. We still need strong groups like the NAACP, Operation PUSH, and the Nation of Islam, but at the end of each of these groups' rainbow, there needs to be a strong lobbying effort if we are going to make change in this country."

Hashim Shomari, a former aide for a U.S. senator from New Jersey and author of *From the Underground: Hip-Hop Culture as an Agent of Social Change*, agrees. "We can't sit on the sidelines. That is one of the important things that the civil rights and Black power movements have taught us," he says. "We won't be in a position to make laws that we want or to actualize political power unless we use the political power that we already have. We might not get everything we want, but if we get in the battle, we'll get something. The question is do we in the hip-hop generation have the political savvy to get out there and fight for what's ours? If not, somebody else will. And don't be surprised when you see your tax dollars funding Ku Klux Klan–type activities."

If Muhammad and Shomari are even partially correct, what is needed is a political organization to place this generation's agenda in part or whole at the center of its program. This is what many young Blacks are in search of, and they have for the most part given up on the old-guard organizations' ability or willingness to produce it. Such an organization would most certainly encourage hundreds of thousands of young Blacks to participate in mainstream politics and the public policy process and would give them a voice in government at the local and national levels.

Perhaps the most effective means of getting such an effort off the ground would be to establish a youth coalition, lobby, or issue advocacy group in the same vein as the Christian Coalition, an organization founded in 1989. Throughout the 1990s, under founder and president Pat Robertson and then director Ralph Reed, the Christian Coalition effectively organized a voting bloc of radical right Christians and moved them to get more involved in the political process. At its height in the mid-1990s, the group claimed more than 2 million members and had a tremendous impact in a very short time span in terms of getting government to be responsive to their needs as conservative Christians.

Similar to the radical Christian right, Black youth could create a voting bloc through voter registration and education organized around the hip-hop generation's political agenda. Such a coalition or lobby group could serve as the advocate for Black youth causes by assuring candidates that it can deliver the Black youth voting bloc, by assuring candidates that rap artists and other young entertainers will financially support candidates that get behind our issues, and by assuring young Black voters that collectively we can make candidates in local and national elections responsive and accountable to the hip-hop generation's political agenda.

Such an organization would be beholden to neither political party but would organize Black youth to cast their votes along lines consistent with their issues. An organization of this magnitude could help secure victory on issues that matter to hip-hop generationers, not lead youth to the polls for voting's sake. At the national level, the organization could lobby lawmakers on issues relevant to the hip-hop generation's political agenda. Around the country, the organization could arouse public concern and heighten media attention on issues of police brutality, prison incarceration, unemployment, economic development, and so on, in the same way that Jesse Jackson and Kweisi Mfume turn up the heat on issues that matter to Operation PUSH, the Rainbow Coalition, and the NAACP. At the local level, the Black youth advocacy group could organize young people to bring their political might to bear on school boards, city councils, and legislative issues, just as Black youth organized against Proposition 21 in California and against the anti-loitering ordinance in Chicago.

Of course, such an undertaking would not solve all of the problems of Black America, but it would be a beginning toward establishing a major political organization in our lifetime that would be responsive to our issues. The question now is not "Will rap become a political force?" but "How soon?" Given hip-hop's tremendous influence (as American pop culture and as a $3–4 billion a year force in the music industry), expanding into the political arena is inevitable. But who will emerge as the hip-hop generation's power brokers? This question is critical to whether hip-hop's foray into politics will be about social change for the many or enrichment for the few.

8

THE CHALLENGE OF RAP MUSIC

From Cultural Movement to Political Power

> MR. MAYOR, IMAGINE THIS WAS YOUR BACKYARD
> MR. GOVERNOR, IMAGINE IT'S YOUR KIDS THAT STARVE
> IMAGINE YOUR KIDS GOTTA SLING CRACK TO SURVIVE,
> SWING A MAC TO BE LIVE . . .
> —NAS, "I WANT TO TALK TO YOU"

IN JUNE 2001, RUSH COMMUNICATIONS CEO RUSSELL
Simmons convened a hip-hop summit in New York City.
With the theme "Taking Back Responsibility," the summit focused its agenda on ways to strengthen rap music's growing
influence. The 300 participants included major rap artists
and industry executives as well as politicians, religious and
community leaders, activists, and scholars. Few forces other
than rap music, now one of the most powerful forces in
American popular culture, could bring together such a diverse gathering of today's African American leaders. In
many ways, the summit signaled hip-hop as the definitive
cultural movement of our generation.

As the major cultural movement of our time, hip-hop (its music, fashion, attitude, style, and language) is undoubtedly one of the core influences for young African Americans born between 1965 and 1984. To fully appreciate the extent to which this is true, think back for a moment about the period between the mid-1970s and the early 1980s, before rap became a mainstream phenomenon. Before MTV. Before BET's Rap City. Before the Fresh Prince of Bel Air. Before *House Party* I or II. It is difficult now to imagine Black youth as a nearly invisible entity in American popular culture. But in those days, that was the case. When young Blacks were visible, it was mostly during the six o'clock evening news reports of crime in urban America.

In contrast, today it is impossible not to see young Blacks in the twenty-first century's public square—the public space of television, film, and the Internet. Our images now extend far beyond crime reports. For most of our contemporaries, it's difficult to recall when this was not the case. Because of rap, the voices, images, style, attitude, and language of young Blacks have become central in American culture, transcending geographic, social, and economic boundaries.

To be sure, professional athletes, especially basketball players, have for decades been young, Black, highly visible, and extremely popular. Yet, their success just didn't translate into visibility for young Blacks overall. For one thing, the conservative culture of professional sports, central to their identity, was often at odds with the rebellious vein inherent in the new Black youth culture. While household-name ball players towed the generic "don't do drugs and stay in school" party line, rappers, the emissaries of the new Black youth culture, advocated more anti-establishment slogans like "fuck the police." Such slogans were vastly more in synch with the hard realities facing young Blacks—so much so that as time marched on and hip-hop culture further solidified its place in American popular culture, basketball culture would also come to feel its influence.

Largely because of rap music, one can tune in to the voices and find the faces of America's Black youth at any point in the day. Having proven themselves as marketable entertainers with successful music careers, rappers star in television sit-coms and film and regularly endorse corporate products (such as Lil' Kim—Candies, Missy Elliot—the Gap, and Common, Fat Joe, and the Goodie Mob—Sprite). In the mid-1980s, a handful of corporations began incorporating hip-hop into their advertisement spots. Most were limited to run-of-the-mill product endorsements. By the late 1990s, however, ads incorporating hip-hop—even those promoting traditionally conservative companies—became increasingly steeped in the subtleties of hip-hop culture. Setting the standard with their extremely hip-hop savvy 1994 Voltron campaign, Sprite broke away from the straight-up celebrity endorsement format. Says Coca-Cola global marketing manager Darryl Cobbin, who was on the cutting edge of this advertising strategy: "I wanted to usher in a real authenticity in terms of hip-hop in advertising. We wanted to pay respect to the music *and* the culture. What's important is the value of hip-hop culture, not only as an image, but as a method of communication."

By the late 1990s, advertisers like the Gap, Nike, AT&T, and Sony soon followed suit and incorporated hip-hop's nuances into their advertising campaigns. As a result, the new Black youth culture resonates throughout today's media, regardless of what companies are selling (from soft drinks and footwear to electronics and telecommunications).

Of course, none of this happened overnight. In fact, more important than the commercialization of rap was the less visible cultural movement on the ground in anyhood USA. In rap's early days, before it became a thriving commercial entity, dj party culture provided the backdrop for this off-the-radar cultural movement. What in the New York City metropolitan area took the form of dj battles and MC chants emerged in Chicago as the house party scene, and in D.C. it was go-go. In other regions of the country, the local movement owed its genesis to rap acts like Run DMC, who broke through to a national audience in the early 1980s. In any case, by the mid-1980s, this local or underground movement began to emerge in the form of cliques, crews, collectives, or simply kids getting together primarily to party, but in the process rhyming, dj-ing, dancing, and tagging. Some, by the early 1990s, even moved into activism. In large cities like Chicago, San Francisco, Houston, Memphis, New Orleans, Indianapolis, and Cleveland and even in smaller cities and suburban areas like Battle Creek, Michigan, and Champaign, Illinois, as the '80s turned to the '90s, more and more young Blacks were coming together in the name of hip-hop.

In the early 1980s, the "in" hip-hop fashion for New York City Black youth included Gazelles (glasses), sheepskins and leather bombers (coats), Clarks (shoes), nameplates, and name belts. In terms of language, Five Percenter expressions like "word is bond" were commonplace. These hip-hop cultural expressions in those days were considered bizarre by Black kids from other regions of the country. A student at the University of Pennsylvania at the time, Conrad Muhammad, the hip-hop minister, speaks to this in reminiscing on the National Black Students Unity Conference he organized in 1987:

> Jokers were getting off buses with shower caps on, perms and curls. MTV and BET had not yet played a role in standardizing Black youth culture the way they do today. Young people from different cities weren't all dressing the same way. Brothers and sisters were stepping off buses saying "we're from the University of

Nebraska, Omaha." "We're from University of Min-
nesota." "We're from Cal Long Beach."

But by the early to mid-1990s, hip-hop's commercialized
element had Black kids on the same page, regardless of geographic region. In this hip-hop friendly national environment,
hip-hop designers like Enyce, Mecca, and FUBU were thriving, multi-platinum sales for rap artists were routine (and
dwarfed the 1980s mark of success: gold sales), and hip-hop
expressions like "blowin' up," "representin'," and "keepin' it
real" worked their way into the conversational language of
Black youth around the country. Contrast this to the
mid–1980s when even those deep into hip-hop didn't see the
extent to which a national cultural movement was unfolding.

"Before the Fresh Fest Tour of 1984, few folks were defining hip-hop culture as hip-hop culture," says Hashim
Shomari, author of *From the Underground: Hip-Hop as an
Agent of Social Change*. "That was a relatively 1990s phenomenon." Practitioners like Africa Bambaataa, Grandmaster
Flash, Fab-Five Freddy, Chuck D, and KRS-One were on the
frontlines of those who saw the need to flesh out the definitions. Also, it wasn't until the early 1990s that breakthrough
books like Joseph Eure and James Spady's *Nation-Conscious
Rap* (1991), Michael Gonzales and Havelock Nelson's *Bring
the Noise: A Guide to Rap Music and Hip-Hop Culture* (1991),
and Tricia Rose's *Black Noise: Rap Music and Black Culture in
Contemporary America* (1994) began to discuss hip-hop as an
influential culture that went beyond the commercial.

Without question, rap's national exposure played a key
role in the uniform way in which the local cultural manifestations evolved. More recently, given rap's commercial success,
alongside limited employment options beyond minimum
wage-jobs for young Blacks, hip-hop's cultural movement at
the local level is increasingly marked by an entrepreneurial

element. On the West Coast, East Coast, in southern and northern cities, and in rural and suburban areas in between, young Blacks are pressing their own CDs and selling them "out the trunk" regionally.[1] Many of them are hoping to eventually put their city on the hip-hop map. What all this around the way activity has in common is that kids are tuned in to the same wavelength via hip-hop, some aspiring to be the next Air Jordan of hip-hop, others engaging in what is to them a way of life without commercial popular culture aspirations, and still others tuning in as a basic engagement with the youth culture of our time.

The commercialized element of this cultural movement and the off-the-radar one fuel each other. The underground element provides a steady stream of emerging talent that in turn gets absorbed into commercialization. That new voice and talent again inspires more discussion (about the art form, new styles, trends, language, and larger issues and themes) and more talent at the local level, which later infuses the commercial manifestation of the cultural movement. Case in point: the more recent wave of talent (say, Master P out of New Orleans, Eve from Philly, and Nelly from St. Louis) is similar to the much earlier waves like the Geto Boys out of Houston and Compton's NWA. Those earlier waves of talent (the Geto Boys, NWA, Too Short, E-40,

---

[1]My emphasis here, as throughout the book, is on Black youth—no disrespect to the countless folks of other racial and ethnic groups down with hip-hop. This is not to say that Latino and to a lesser extent Asian and Native American youth have not been influential in and touched by hip-hop culture. Neither is it meant to ignore the distinctiveness of Caribbean Americans. More recently white kids, a large segment of hip-hop's listening audience, are jumping into the fray. Nevertheless, rap music indisputably remains dominated by Black youth in both its commercial and local manifestations.

and others) most certainly provided inspiration for the No Limit Soldiers and Ruff Ryders, who came later. Like the earliest waves of artists, each group represents its distinct region, while tapping into the national movement. In turn, Master P, Eve, and Nelly will influence the next wave of talent breaking from the margins into the mainstream.

It's not exactly a chicken-or-egg question, however. Hip-hop as a culture indisputably emerged in the South Bronx in the late 1970s, and in other parts of the northeast shortly thereafter, before branching out around the country in the early 1980s. What's arguable is the extent to which hip-hop would have become the national cultural movement that it is today without commercialization.

In 1988, rapper Chuck D of the rap group Public Enemy described rap music as "the Black CNN." This was certainly true at the grassroots level at the time. However, the decade of the 1990s proved even more profound as rap music became thoroughly accepted and promoted in mainstream American popular culture. As such, rap provided the foundation for a resounding young Black mainstream presence that went far beyond rap music itself.

Understanding the degree to which the local and commercial are deeply entrenched and interdependent, one can began to grasp the far-reaching effects of hip-hop on young Blacks. As the primary vehicle through which young Blacks have achieved a national voice and presence, rap music transmits the new Black youth culture to a national audience. And in the same way as the mainstream media establishes the parameters for national discussion for the nation at large, rap music sets the tone for Black youth. As the national forum for Black youth concerns and often as the impetus for discussion around those issues, rap music has done more than any one entity to help our generation forge a distinct identity.

Another important aspect of what makes rap so substantive in the lives of young Blacks is its multilingual nature. In addition to beaming out hip-hop culture, rap also conveys elements of street culture, prison culture, and the new Black youth culture. Often all of these elements overlap within rap's lyrics and visual images. In the process, images and ideas that define youth culture for this generation—such as designer clothes, like Sean Jean, Phat Farm, and Tommy Hilfiger, ever-changing styles of dress, and local colloquialisms—are beamed out to a captive national audience. Also transmitted are cues of personal style, from cornrows and baby dreads to body piercing and tattoos.

And finally, even more important than fashion, style, and language, the new Black culture is encoded within the images and lyrics of rap and thus help define what it means to be young and Black at the dawn of the millennium. In the process, rap music has become the primary vehicle for transmitting culture and values to this generation, relegating Black families, community centers, churches, and schools to the back burner.

To be sure, rap marked a turning point, a shift from practically no public voice for young Blacks—or at best an extremely marginalized one—to Black youth culture as the rage in mainstream popular culture. And more than just increasing Black youth visibility, rap articulated publicly and on a mass scale many of this generation's beliefs, relatively unfiltered by the corporate structures that carried it. Even when censored with bleeps or radio-friendly "clean" versions, the messages were consistent with the new Black youth culture and more often than not struck a chord with young Blacks, given our generation's unique collective experiences. At the same time, the burgeoning grassroots arts movement was underway. All was essential to rap's movement into the mainstream and its emergence as the paramount cultural movement of our time.

Although hip-hop has secured its place as a cultural movement, its biggest challenge lies ahead. In the late 1980s when gangsta rap first emerged, community activists and mainstream politicians of the civil rights generation began to challenge rap's content. This criticism forced a dialogue that revealed one of the Black community's best kept secrets, the bitter generational divide between hip-hop generationers and our civil rights/Black power parents.

The key concern was Black cultural integrity: how have the very public images of young Blacks in hip-hop music and culture affected the larger Black community? Central to this discussion was the pervasive use of offensive epithets in rap lyrics, such as "nigga," "bitch," and "ho," all of which reinforce negative stereotypes about Blacks. What was the price of this remarkable breakthrough in the visibility of young Blacks in the mainstream culture? Had young rappers simply transferred images of young Black men as criminals from news reports to entertainment? And finally, had the growing visibility of young Black entertainers further marginalized young Black intellectuals and writers, who have remained nearly invisible?

A handful of responses emerged. The response from the rap industry was unanimous: free speech is a constitutional right. The predominant response from rap artists themselves was a proverbial head in the sand. Most reasoned that the older generation was out of touch with the concerns of hip-hop generationers. Just as our parents' generation was unfamiliar with the music, the thinking went, when it came to other matters of our generation, particularly issues involving hip-hop, they, likewise, didn't know what they were talking about. By and large, the question of rap's attack on Black cultural integrity went unaddressed. In fact, the use of incendiary words like "nigga" and "bitch" has become so commonplace in rap's lyrics that today even those in rap's growing white audience routinely use them when referring to each other and often their Black peers (a matter Spike Lee vaguely touched on in the film *Bamboozled*).

Lately, as the theme of the Simmons summit "Taking Back Responsibility" suggests, hip-hop is again undertaking the critical task of questioning its relationship to the community. David Mays, publisher of the hip-hop magazine *The Source*, and Reverend Al Sharpton held a series of summits eight months prior to the Simmons summit, which called for a code of conduct in light of arrests of numerous rappers and the growing association of rappers with criminality. Minister Conrad Muhammad, dubbed the hip-hop minister for the moral voice he's long brought to the hip-hop community, felt the Mays-Sharpton gathering didn't go far enough. Muhammad called for a summit of Black rap artists, rap industry executives, and activists to discuss ways of holding the hip-hop industry accountable to the Black community. Appalled by Muhammad's moral challenge to the rap industry, Simmons countered Muhammad with a call for his own summit to be held within a few weeks of the Muhammad one.

Simmons, a major player in the rap industry who earlier began flexing his political muscle by reaching out to Democratic Party insiders like Hillary Clinton in her bid for the U.S. Senate, brought together the largest and most media-celebrated summit to date. Joining rap industry insiders were African American notables like minister Louis Farrakhan, NAACP-head Kweisi Mfume, U.S. Representative Cynthia McKinney, and scholars Cornel West and Michael Eric Dyson.

The Simmons event was impressive in terms of sheer numbers and diverse backgrounds. But where it most seriously came up short was in its failure to incorporate the grassroots segment of hip-hop's cultural movement, especially hip-hop generation activists. When hip-hop's true influence as a cultural movement is finally understood, events like these will recognize that the very same synergy at the heart of hip-hop's commercial success has also informed our generation's activists and political theorists. Just as some record executives can give us a blueprint for blowin' up rap acts, the ideas that our generation's activists hold about maximizing rap's potential for social change have been seasoned in their day-to-day work and experience. If our generation's cultural movement is to evolve to have a meaningful political impact, the local segments of hip-hop's cultural movement —from hip-hop generation activists to local entrepreneurs to the everyday hip-hop kids on the block—must not only be brought to the table, but must have a major voice.

Furthermore, rather than centering the discussion within our own generation—*and*, yes, including the expertise and insight of our parents' generation—the invitation-only Simmons summit turned to the mostly liberal-integrationist civil rights leadership and music industry executives. The result was predictable: a combination of the traditional music industry call for free speech, which allows for continued blockbuster sales without disrupting the minstrel-esque proven formula for success, and the traditional civil rights activist call for young voters to support Democratic candidates for public office. Neither of these same-game-with-another-name reforms challenge civil righters or industry insiders to do anything different than what they are already doing. Moreover, pushing activists of the civil rights generation to the forefront of this effort is tantamount to casting older-generation R&B singers like Dionne Warwick and Lionel Richie as leads in a 'hood film or featuring them at a concert alongside ODB or Lil' Kim.

Until hip-hop is recognized as a broad cultural movement, rather than simply an influential moneymaker, those who seek to tap into hip-hop's potential to impact social change should not expect substantive progress. A unified front between hip-hop's commercial and grassroots sectors on the issue of sociopolitical action would change the nature of the dialogue. For example, in the same way that the hip-hop community through its cultural movement inherently answered the question, "what is hip-hop culture?" a new inclusive framework inevitably would answer the question, "what do we mean by politicizing the hip-hop generation?" Is our goal to run hip-hop generationers for office, to turn out votes for Democrats and Republicans, to form a third party, or to provide our generation with a more concrete political education?

Indications of the endless possibilities of this unified front approach are evident in the following examples of rap's demonstrated success in extending its influence beyond popular culture.

The Haitian Refugee Crisis.   In April 1997, the Fugees held a concert in Port-au-Prince, Haiti, to raise money for local charities and to bring international media attention to the economic and political plight of Haiti's people. Financed mostly by Wyclef Jean, the event was also supported by local companies. Unfortunately, the effort got caught between U.S. foreign policy and the type of corruption that has come to plague new governments on the heels of dictators. As a result, the funds raised never reached the intended charities. Shortly before the event, the Haitian government took control of the fundraiser, including handling all receipts. Afterward they issued a report declaring that the event only broke even. The event did succeed in gaining media attention, however. Beyond that, it demonstrated one way that successful American entertainers can support larger international causes.

Rappers and Mumia Abu-Jamal.   One of the major issues of our time has been the disproportionate representation of African Americans in both the penal system and on death row. This issue is critical to a generation that during its lifetime has seen the Black prison population increase from fewer than 250,000 to nearly 1 million. Mumia Abu-Jamal's fight for justice brought the issue to the fore. Abu-Jamal was convicted in 1982 for the murder of Daniel Faulkner, a white Philadelphia cop. He and Faulkner were shot while Abu-Jamal was attempting to break up a confrontation between his brother and the officer. Abu-Jamal was later sentenced to death. Supporters say the former Black Panther was railroaded by a racist police department and received an unfair trial. Abu-Jamal insists that he did not commit the crime and says that he is being punished for his politics. The rap community's participation in Abu-Jamal's fight for justice persists in rap lyrics, in support at rallies, and at anti–death penalty benefits. KRS-One, Channel Live, and other rappers have been among Abu-Jamal's supporters. As a result of these efforts, few hip-hop generation kids are unfamiliar with Abu-Jamal's fight for justice. Most have an opinion on the death penalty and are aware of the inconsistencies in American justice for Blacks and whites.

The Million Man March.   The Million Man March was the largest mass gathering in the history of the country. Young

Blacks turned out in huge numbers partly because rappers have made it fashionable for Blacks of this generation to support Black causes. Furthermore, rappers like Ice Cube, Ice T, Puff Daddy, Das EFX, Common Sense, and others strongly supported the event. This certainly helped to heighten the importance of the march in the minds of young Blacks.

The Million Youth March. At the eleventh hour, the Million Youth March languished under various obstacles that seemed destined to sabotage the event. Responding to some of the needs to pull the event off, Master P made a major donation to the event that helped the show to go on. As contributions from hip-hop generation athletes and entertainers to larger causes remain few and far between, the gesture was a much needed breath of fresh air. In 1998, Danny Glover made a $1 million contribution to TransAfrica, the Washington, D.C.–based organization that lobbies on behalf of U.S. foreign policy toward Africa and the Caribbean Basin. Financial support from the hip-hop community for serious political efforts remains rare. Master P's support for the Million Youth March is an example of how rap artists can make the difference to such efforts.

East Coast/West Coast Conflict. Probably no other event in rap's history has received as much coverage in the mainstream media as the so-called East Coast/West Coast beef—imagined and real antagonism between rappers and fans on the East Coast (mostly New York City) and the West Coast (mostly rappers and fans in Los Angeles). The conflict, which in print often centered on rap labels Death Row and Bad Boy, climaxed with the gangland-style murders of Tupac Shakur in 1996 and Biggie Smalls in 1997. In the wake of their deaths, many rappers participated in efforts to end the seemingly out-of-control antagonisms. From a rapper summit called by Louis Farrakhan's Nation of Islam to rap lyrics denouncing the East-West feud, rappers like Nas, Jay-Z, Common, Snoop, and others succeeded in reducing East-West antagonism.

Social Programs and Foundations. Several rappers have founded social programs and foundations to give back to the communities that produced them; among them are the Wu Charitable Foundation, Camp Cool J, the Refugee Project, Christopher Wallace Foundation, and the Tupac Amaru Shakur Memorial Foundation. All of these organizations focus their efforts on urban youth who lack opportunities and access. Few venture far beyond the typical feel-good effort that boosts the celebrity's publicity. However, some of these programs have features that encourage community responsibility and participation. For example, Daddy's House Social Programs, Sean "P-Diddy" Combs' seven-year-old program for children aged 6–16, sponsors a Saturday school that teaches regular academic courses as well as manhood/womanhood training for teens. Daddy's House also sends a group of children to Ghana and South Africa as part of an Urban Youth Tour. In return, each student makes a presentation to their respective communities when they return home. Lauryn Hill's Refugee Project conducts a mentorship program where each child is assigned two mentors (a college student and a professional). In addition, Camp Hill, the Refugee Project's summer camp, has a required family day component built into the two-week camp, which parents of campers must attend. The Tupac Amaru Shakur Memorial Foundation helps former inmates who are single-parent mothers make the transition back to society. These are examples of community efforts that rappers have supported with their recently acquired wealth. These efforts can serve as a cornerstone for even greater, more cooperative efforts.

Most of the activities concerned with social change have taken place outside of the limelight of rap's growing popularity. In some cases, the activity may seem superficial, but careful examination reveals that some rappers individually and collectively have consistently responded to issues important to this generation. The response may not have always been effective, or even politically correct, but these are the types of activities that have galvanized community-building efforts. The extent of the impact seems to be directly proportionate to the degree that such efforts work themselves deeper into the fabric of hip-hop's cultural movement.

Rap music's ability to influence social change should not be taken lightly. The U.S. Department of Health and Human Services reported that rates of teen pregnancy fell by 4 percent in 1997 and that rates decreased by 17 percent in the 1990s overall. Social policy has had very little impact on this and related issues in the lives of America's poor. In many cases, social policy has only exacerbated the problems. Experts have offered numerous explanations for the decline, but none have considered rap music a factor. Perhaps rap music's influence as a transmitter of ideas should be more carefully considered.

At least one team of researchers at Emory University's Rollins School of Public Health agrees. In a recent study, they found that after Black boys and girls 11–14 years old listened to rappers like Big Pun, the Goodie Mob, and Lil' Kim, they were more knowledgeable about AIDS and were better prepared to discuss safe sex, condom use, and abstinence. "The knowledge they gain about themselves and the disease helps kids make informed decisions about sexual behavior and makes them less likely to engage in risky sexual practices," said Torrence Stephens, lead author of the study. This study adds to the growing body of evidence that hip-hop is much more than entertainment.

In each of these efforts, there is an *informal* exchange between hip-hop's commercial and grassroots sectors. A *formal* unified front could effect even greater change. Here are a few other ways that a unified front could begin to expand rap's influence into social and political arenas.

First, a unified front of rap artists, industry insiders, hip-hop generation activists, and everyday kids on the block could begin to challenge rap's ever-growing listening audience of white youth. How can that relationship build on America's unkept promise of inclusion? If this engagement with Black youth culture is more than simply a fleeting fascination, what will it take to motivate white youth to make the transition from simply enjoying and interacting with hip-hop to using their own power and influence to enhance the quality of American race relations?

In an April 5, 2001, *New York Times* article titled "Pressed Against a 'Race Ceiling,'" Black elected officials lamented the difficulty they have getting elected to statewide office where majority-white populations won't vote for them, a sentiment expressed by New Orleans Mayor Marc Morial in his comments to the *Times*: "People have asked, 'Wouldn't you like to run for the Senate, for governor or attorney general?' And I say, 'Certainly, I'd be interested in that at some point. But in Louisiana they haven't elected a statewide African-American official since the 1880s.'"

Since the passage of the Voting Rights Act of 1965, only one African American has been elected governor and only two have been elected to the U.S. Senate. If rap's white listening audience translated its familiarity and interest in Black youth culture to their voting habits and challenged their parents to deal with the continuing racial contradictions as well, this glass ceiling would be obliterated, and race relations as we know them would never be the same.

Second, young white movers and shakers within the rap industry could be challenged by a unified front to use their knowledge and insight to further narrow the racial divide not only inside the industry but outside of it. Insisting on multi-ethnic hires and diversified staffing in the industry, rather than hiding behind the old excuse "we can't find any qualified ones," and insisting on equal and fair pay across the board would be a good start. Likewise, challenging stereotypical and degrading practices, images, and lyrics in the rap industry is a must.

Third, a unified front could challenge successful rap artists to explore ways of pooling their resources and influence to lead and assist community rebuilding and economic revitalization efforts in poor communities. Activists from the civil rights generation challenged large corporations that do a significant amount of business with African Americans to support development within those communities; a unified front between commercial and around the way hip-hop could do the same. The seemingly endless list of companies marketing products to young Blacks through hip-hop's influence (from those whose ads lace rap music magazines and those who sponsor awards shows to rap labels themselves) should be challenged to reciprocate by supporting community development projects. Such efforts would contribute to and strengthen Black community development and further endear artists to fans. Local community activists will support these efforts to the degree that they improve the day-to-day lives of community residents.

Recently, the Church of God in Christ in West Los Angeles finished building a new $60 million sanctuary with the help of members, who include several major Black entertainers; with their support, a vision became a reality. In another effort, the 2000 Watts Foundation created by MTV vj and R&B singer Tyrese is bringing together corporate sponsors to build a community center in Watts, Tyrese's hometown. Efforts like these provide models for future projects.

Fourth, a united front could challenge the rap industry to finally resolve the issue of hip-hop's responsibility to Black cultural integrity. Rappers like Chuck D, Queen Latifah, Lauryn Hill, Will Smith, and Common have long tried to raise the bar on lyrical content. Community activists like C. Delores Tucker and Calvin Butts and more recently Conrad Muhammad have challenged rap artists and the industry to do more to make socially responsible lyrics as pervasive in hip-hop as those that advance stereotypes. Along with the mainstreaming of rap throughout the 1990s, elements of street culture and prison culture have become more and more dominant in rap lyrics, compounding the now decade-old problem of stereotypical images in hip-hop.

Just as problematic is hip-hop's growing tendency to cross over into the adult entertainment industry—from the soft porn images of rap music videos and the XXX hip-hop video *Doggystyle* (a Snoop Dogg/Larry Flynt joint venture) to emerging magazines like *Black Gold* that blur the lines between pornography and hip-hop. Not only is hip-hop a major force in the lives of hip-hop generationers at the older end of the age group, but it also heavily impacts those at the younger end of the spectrum, some of whom are just approaching their teenage years. The commercial rap industry must begin to more seriously weigh the impact of exposing children to age-inappropriate (adult) situations. A unified front could develop workable approaches for addressing these issues. As Muhammad and Simmons squared off, Bill Stepheney, political activist and CEO of Stepson Media, put it succinctly in his comments to the *New York Post* (May 8, 2001): "What is the line that we [artists and industry executives] are unwilling to cross for profits. Is there a line? Or is it completely laissez-faire?"

Finally, the "Taking Back Responsibility" summit should be applauded for advocating artist development. Much more can and should be done in this area. An ongoing alliance between those in the commercial industry and those at the grassroots level would inevitably build on the Black community's traditional call for self-determination through greater Black ownership, control, and influence within the industry beyond being "the show." The current generation of rap industry insiders needs to develop a new generation of songwriters, performers, and music industry executives with real power and ownership within the industry. Kalamu Ya Salaam, activist-poet and former executive director of the New Orleans Jazz and Heritage Foundation, identified this need as part of the solution to America's long-standing race problem. In his *What Is Life: Reclaiming the Black Blues Self* (Third World Press, 1994), he proposes the music industry as an important sector for Black economic development:

> A current possible solution is what I call horizontal economic development at a mass level in a specific economic sector. The traditional vertical mode of economic development is simply individual wealth generated by climbing the earnings ladder in a given field. The miscellaneous array of athletes and entertainers celebrated in *Ebony* and *Black Enterprise* are a prime example of this in our community. . . . African Americans must make a concerted effort to carve out a significant niche

in the ... music business. ... It offers the broadest array of opportunities for a diversity of skill areas while remaining focused in a particular economic sector. ... The music business is one of the few segments of the modern American economy in which [African Americans] have any significant leverage. ...

The real challenge of integration is to capture control of economic development. We are the creative labor of a significant portion of the music industry. Now is the time to become the controllers of the fruit of our labor. African Americans desperately need economic development and a move on the music industry is a feasible route. We make the music. Now, let's make the money.

A working unified front would greatly enhance rap's potential to contribute to needed sociopolitical transformations. The real question is this: why should hip-hop generationers continue to participate in and support a multibillion dollar industry if it fails to in any way address the critical problems facing our generation? What good is rap music if it does nothing more than give young Blacks the opportunity to "dance to our own degradation" (as Black studies scholar Maulana Karenga has noted) and if it enriches only a few at the expense of the many? If rap is to stand as not only the most significant cultural movement of our time but one of history's most salient, and I believe it will, hip-hop generationers both inside and outside of the rap music industry must rise to the challenge. All the components for a mass political movement in our lifetime are in place and functioning—but separate. Do we dare join them together?

INDEX

Powell, Kevin, 95, 99

Pride, black, 8

Prisons

and black sprituality, 81–83

and the decline of black political power, 80–81

effect on families, 77–78

and HIV/AIDS, 79–80

influence on black youth culture, 76–77

and mental health, 80

privatization of, 71–76

and society's view of blacks, 79–80

Public Enemy, 167

Publishing, black-oriented, 5, 8–9

Puff Daddy, 46, 208

Queen Latifah, 5, 131, 176–177, 213

R. Kelly, 105

Race

and activism, 148–149

and employment, 35–37

and racial profiling, 65–66

Race Matters, 10

Racketeering Influenced Corrupt Organization Act, 54

Rage in Harlem, A, 123

Rage of a Privileged Class, The, 13

Raical profiling, 65–66

Raising Fences: A Black Man's Love Story, 95

Rangel, Charles, 180

Rape, 97–106

Rap music

artists, 4, 11, 47, 104, 199–204

commercialization of, 123, 200–202

and the East Coast/West Coast conflict, 208–209

and the hip-hop culture, 4–6, 8, 9–10, 197–198

and politics, 176–177

and social programs and foundations, 209–211

and women, 85–87, 104

Rap Pages, 5, 176

Rappers Educating All Curricula through Hip-Hop (REACH), 161

Rap the Vote, 176, 188–190

Rauf, Mahmoud Abdul, 152

Reed, Ralph, 192

Reeves, Jimmie Lynn, 38

Reeves, Shannon, 151, 167–169, 178

Reid, Frank, 158

Reparations, 25–26, 179–180

Republican Party, the, 150, 167–169, 183–187

Republic of New Afrika, 25

Reyes, Daniel, 65